Judaism and Human Rights in Contemporary Thought

Recent Titles in
Bibliographies and Indexes in Religious Studies

Judaism and Human Rights in Contemporary Thought

A Bibliographical Survey

S. Daniel Breslauer

Bibliographies and Indexes in Religious Studies, Number 25
G.E. Gorman, Advisory Editor

Greenwood Press
Westport, Connecticut • London

Library of Congress Cataloging-in-Publication Data

Breslauer, S. Daniel.
   Judaism and human rights in contemporary thought : a
bibliographical survey / S. Daniel Breslauer.
      p.   cm.—(Bibliographies and indexes in religious studies,
   ISSN 0742-6836 ; no. 25)
   Includes bibliographical references and indexes.
   ISBN 0-313-27994-2
   1. Human rights—Religious aspects—Judaism. 2. Ethics, Jewish.
3. Judaism—Doctrines. 4. Judaism—20th century.   I. Title.
II. Series.
BM645.H85B74   1993
296.3'877—dc20   92-38996

British Library Cataloguing in Publication Data is available.

Library of Congress Catalog Card Number: 92-38996
ISBN: 0-313-27994-2
ISSN: 0742-6836

First published in 1993

Greenwood Press, 88 Post Road West, Westport, CT 06881
An imprint of Greenwood Publishing Group, Inc.

Printed in the United States of America

The paper used in this book complies with the
Permanent Paper Standard issued by the National
Information Standards Organization (Z39.48-1984).

10 9 8 7 6 5 4 3 2 1

Contents

Foreword

...What is it that God asks of you?
Only to act justly, to love loyalty, to
walk wisely before your God.

Micah 6:8

...In two respects Judaic tradition
can make a contribution to natural
law and by that token to the life and
thought of our age. The first is the
dynamism of the Hebrew vision of
life and history, which is
fundamental to the prophets of
Israel. The second is the passionate
concern for justice, freedom and
peace that characterized the biblical
legislators, prophets and sages, as
well as their rabbinic successors.

Robert Gordis, *Judaic Ethics for a
Lawless World*

It is often this "passionate concern for justice" that liberals of other faiths, or of
none, find most appealing about Judaism; it is certainly a concern in desperately
short supply at the present time, as the world exhibits one of its periodic swings
back to the "greed is good" ethic espoused by Gordon Gekko in the film, *Wall
Street*. Perhaps this ethic has always existed in the West, having merely been
couched in more acceptable terms at different times. In the present age economic
determinism has long held sway, coloring our understanding not only of economics
and commerce but also of society, politics, and basic human needs. As Alan

Storkey views this economic dogma, it was "...a process of enslavement whereby people were brought into bondage by the forces created by naturalism."[1] And such enslavement is not something of a remote, nineteenth century past — it has occurred in America and Britain with all but the complete destruction of a genuine social welfare system, and it now seems to be happening in countries as disparate as Russia and Australia.

In *Transforming Economics* Storkey suggests that the economy has long been our idol, with Samuelson, Lipsey, and others its prophets and soothsayers. We are now, Storkey believes, poised to move beyond this idolatry into an objective evaluation of economic and social responsibility, "the era of naturalistic and positivistic economics should now be at an end, to be replaced by a more self-critical evaluation of our economic activity and its failings."[2] While this *should* be the case, is it really occurring? In the world's most powerful economies, especially Germany, Japan, and the USA, there seems to be a marked resurgence of economic conservatism, accompanied by a social rationalism that overrides any ethical conscience or sense of human justice. "Poverty, illness, squalor, these are regarded as just punishment for the failures in society, who by definition are sinners."[3] The legacy of Reagan and Thatcher has reverberated around the world, with the narrow-minded and selfish middle classes closing ranks and seeking to insulate themselves from the realities of economic and social injustice.

Yet Robert Gordis reminds us that "the right to justice adheres in all men, whatever their origin or racial character. The right and duty to enjoy God's world and its blessings are inalienable, having been conferred on them by God and not by the state or a social contract."[4] One of the enduring messages of Judaism — and of its offspring, Christianity — through the ages has been this, that inalienable human rights are to be protected and not abrogated; this is articulated through a system of ethical principles and rules of morality. As Daniel Breslauer has reminded us elsewhere, in Judaism ethics and morality are closely linked. "Judaism has ... both an ethics (a set of broad principles establishing moral

---

[1]   Alan Storkey, *Transforming Economics: A Christian Way to Employment*. Third Way Books (London: SPCK, 1986), p. 196.

[2]   *Ibid.*

[3]   Robert Gordis, *Judaic Ethics for a Lawless World*. Moreshet Series. Studies in Jewish History, Literature and Thought, 12 (New York: Jewish Theological Seminary of America, 1986), p. 100.

[4]   *Ibid.*, p. 76.

priorities) and a morality (a set of specific rules of behavior to apply to concrete cases)."[5] In the present context this suggests that Judaism concerns itself with the elimination of misery and suffering caused by men; it does this through an ethical system involving humanitarian rules of conduct that are based on that simple yet difficult rule, "do not do to anyone what you hate." The prophet Micah states this rule more positively as "act justly," and the appropriate actions are specified by many biblical writers and commentators. Thus pentateuchal law in Exodus and Deuteronomy demands justice for all, including slaves, strangers, widows, women, orphans, the poor, enemies, even animals.

The rules of morality arising from the requirement to act justly are derived from a set of basic religious affirmations set forth in the first chapter of Genesis. First, all life is holy. Second, humanity is fashioned in the image of God. Third, human beings rule the created world. Fourth, the world is good. These and similar affirmations are important for two reasons. At the theoretical level attributing the origin of life to God inculcates, in Breslauer's words, "a theory of a predictable natural world in which the just regime is one that is hospitable to that nature" (p.5). At a more practical level humanity has special responsibility to order society so that it promotes the well-being of its members and thwarts such dehumanizing attitudes as selfishness, cruelty, greed, and hatred.

It is our view, in other words, that Judaism possesses both an ethical theory of justice and humanitarianism and rules of morality regarding human rights. This theory, articulated as ethical principles and moral practices, has its origins in the Hebrew Bible and the Talmud. As Breslauer affirms in the opening chapter of this work, "the Bible certainly contains injunctions concerning interhuman behavior — the ten commandments, the laws in Exodus, Leviticus, and Deuteronomy all emphasize humanistic concerns. The legal material of the Talmud and its development in later rabbinic thinking provides valuable instruction concerning the protection of life, property, and personal freedom" (p. 7). Of course, no one would argue that a mere listing of injunctions or rules of conduct constitutes a theory of human rights. However, according to the Jewish tradition, these rules and injunctions are derived from the will of God, and it is this derivation that subsequently forms the basis for such a theory.

The divine imperative, coupled with recognition of the basic dignity of humanity, has provided a unique foundation for the articulation of a specifically Jewish approach to human rights in both theory and practice. This has occurred gradually over the centuries, especially through commentaries of the great rabbis in the Middle Ages and treatises of Jewish philosophers in the Enlightenment.

---

[5] S. Daniel Breslauer, *Contemporary Jewish Ethics: A Bibliographical Survey.* Bibliographies and Indexes in Religious Studies, 6 (Westport, CT: Greenwood Press, 1985), p. 7.

During our own century the development has been largely contextual, with Jewish thinkers relating the theory and practice of human rights to the Holocaust, Zionism and other events. The story of the Jews in history is a uniquely shameful catalogue of the abrogation of human rights by Western society. The irony of this is that our Western practice of human rights has its origin largely in the Jewish tradition, and each time these rights are trampled it is likely to be a Jewish commentator who reminds us of our sin. It is not just in the "classic" areas of freedom of conscience and social equality that Judaism makes a contribution, but in aspects of human rights that characterize the latter half of the twentieth century as well — women's rights, the Right to Life Movement, privacy, racism. All of these have been addressed from the perspective of Judaism, and all of them benefit from the application of Jewish ethical principles and moral rules.

There is, then, a long and important tradition of Jewish attention to human rights in theory and practice. This has resulted in a corpus of literature that offers significant insights for both Jews and non-Jews. "As the present bibliography shows, a wealth of literature written by and about Jews as a vehicle for reflections about human rights enriches the discussion about the theoretical and practical implications of the idea of human rights..." (p. 4). It is especially for this reason that we approached Dr. Daniel Breslauer, Professor of Religious Studies at the University of Kansas, to prepare a volume that would document the development and trends in Judaism and human rights. In a sense this volume is a logical extension of Professor Breslauer's earlier contributions to this series: *Contemporary Jewish Ethics: A Bibliographical Survey* (1985) and *Modern Jewish Morality: A Bibliographical Survey* (1986). The first volume presents a thematic approach to the ethical principles and theories of modern Judaism, while the second focuses on modern Jewish moral reflection as seen through six "crises" of the human life cycle. In this third volume he extends the bibliographic study of modern Jewish morality to the sphere of human rights.

With this compilation Dr. Breslauer confirms his pre-eminence among bibliographers of modern Jewish ethics and morality. The appropriateness of this statement may be found in the following pages, which I am pleased to commend for four reasons. First, the five part introductory survey both places the subsequent bibliography in context and summarizes the various arguments and schools related to human rights as a clearly defined component in Judaism. Any student seeking to understand Jewish ethics and morality should read this essay together with the essays in Professor Breslauer's earlier bibliographic studies. Second, the entries in this bibliography manage to treat not only the biblical and talmudic origins of human rights but also the many subsequent theories of human rights found in Judaism. Third, Breslauer has selected for specific treatment seventeen aspects of human rights that are both representative of Jewish thinking in this field and also most significant to modern society, from equality and minority rights to such basic human needs as health and employment. Fourth, the annotations are descriptive and evaluative in an enviously economic style that directs users to the most appropriate sources clearly and succinctly.

Professor Breslauer has managed to combine these attributes in a single volume with his usual careful and unflappable scholarship. From personal experience I know that such work is a sure avenue to eccentricity, yet from afar Dan Breslauer appears to have escaped this illness. The result is a careful and judicious survey that is both accessible to the student and useful to the scholar. It is commendable not only for its broad treatment of the various aspects of Judaism and human rights but also for its logical arrangement and clear assessment of the most important publications in the field. In short, this work continues Daniel Breslauer's high bibliographic standard in treating topics of Jewish ethics and morality. As such, it is a most welcome addition to his earlier volumes in Bibliographies and Indexes in Religious Studies.

The Revd Dr. G.E. Gorman FLA FRSA
Advisory Editor
Charles Sturt University — Riverina
Australia

Preface

Several works by such publishers as Human Rights Watch, Amnesty International, Israeli publishers including the Ministry of Affairs, Betzelem, and the Organization of Human Rights in Israel, many Arab nations, and the Palestine Liberation Organization, detail conduct relative to human rights in Israel and the territories taken during various Arab-Israeli wars. These texts provide important background to any discussion of human rights in Israel. This bibliography, however, emphasizes human rights in *Judaism* and is therefore as interested in theoretical discussions about the nature and substance of human rights as in the practical application of that theory either by Jews or to Jews. Because of that orientation, I have focused on those books and articles which use the concrete data as the basis for generalizing about Jewish views of human rights. This bibliography also excludes several other types of material of relevance to the subject matter. Numerous Ph.D. and M.A. dissertations focus on the topic of religion and human rights. These are not included in the bibliography. Many, often well prepared, audio-visual aids such as audio and video cassettes bring the issues and reality concerning violations of human rights into concrete images. Because this bibliography is meant primarily for scholars working in religious ethics, these aids have been excluded.

This volume begins with an introductory chapter summarizing and explaining the basic concerns found in the entries that follow. These entries are drawn from scholarly books and journals in the fields of Hebrew Bible, Jewish religion, Jewish ethics, and Jewish politics. Scholars researching the modern theory of human rights and those seeking its roots in older classical traditions will find the entries of value. The modern discussion of human rights actually begins after World War II, and Jews have a particular interest in the subject. While Judaism's biblical roots provide an important resource for developing a theory of human rights, Jewish experience in the Nazi Holocaust stimulated interest in generating such a theory at all. The modern dilemmas faced by Jews particularly in the former Soviet Union and in the State of Israel, but also in the United States, have encouraged Jewish reflection on this question.

This bibliography surveys the variety of thinking on this topic in modern discussions from the early period of Jewish emancipation into modernity in the eighteenth century, through the most recent debates about Jewish politics in the Middle East. The bibliography, however, also includes a historical section, drawing together studies of biblical and rabbinic views of human rights. The majority of works included are written in Hebrew or English, but relevant studies, primarily in French and German, have also been included. Works included either take Jews or Judaism as their subject matter or are written by Jews expressing a self-consciously "Jewish" perspective. Since academic reflection on the theory of universal human rights really begins after the end of World War II, most entries span 1950 to the present. Because that reflection often includes meditation on earlier visions of human rights, secondary material concerning the Enlightenment generally, and the Jewish Enlightenment in particular are used. Very little secondary literature, however, focuses on how Zionists used the language of human rights to defend their vision of Judaism. This lack explains the inclusion in this bibliography of several early twentieth century Zionist thinkers who utilized the terminology of human rights in their thought. This bibliography is meant to be used by scholars working in the philosophy of human rights and in modern Jewish intellectual history. While some seminal articles appeared in more popular journals such as *Judaism* (entry 037), the majority of works culled here are chosen for their contribution to scholarly research.

The book divides into an Introductory Survey and five chapters. The Introductory Survey, linked to the bibliography by cross references, analyzes the problems involved in studying Judaism and human rights, sketches the classical sources of Jewish thinking on human rights, the specific rights generated by Jewish theory, and the modern dilemmas facing Jews seeking to make moral choices concerning human rights. Several of the decisions made in this volume may be controversial (for example, the decision to consider Karl Marx as an exponent of a Jewish theory of human rights). The Introductory Survey explains the basis for these decisions and defends them in the context of the project at hand.

The first chapter scans anthologies and bibliographies to discern the resources available to the general reader. These works provide easily obtainable information about Jews and human rights and Jewish thinking about human rights. A glance at this chapter should show the reader the problems attendant to a study of Judaism and human rights, problems to be described in detail in the Introductory Survey. In the light of the necessity to describe and delimit these problems, certain bibliographies are included despite their absence of reference to Jewish views. These bibliographies highlight the neglect commonly given to Jewish involvement in creating a theory of human rights. Since few bibliographies on human rights include the primary journals in which studies on Jewish matters occur, a short selection of these periodicals appears in this second chapter.

The second chapter investigates the classical sources of Jewish thinking on human rights. This chapter collects books and articles treating human rights as considered in the Hebrew Bible and the rabbinic literature. In one way this chapter overlaps chapter four that enumerates specific rights protected by a Jewish theory of human rights. Several entries in this chapter turn to the classical sources of Judaism, especially the Hebrew Bible and the Talmud, to illuminate such particular concerns as family rights, individual rights, medical rights, the right to life, and the rights of women. The basic focus of the chapter, however, is on whether these classical sources do indeed provide instruction for modern theorists of human rights.

The third chapter focuses on Jewish theories of human rights generally, rather than in relationship to specific rights. Whether considering modern Jewish history, the classical sources of Jewish thought, or generalizing from the study of a specific issue of human rights, contemporary theorists disagree as to whether Judaism even contains a theory of human rights, and those who think that it does differ greatly in their understanding of it. This chapter collects material that either directly or indirectly reflects on the question as to the presence of a theory of human rights in Judaism. The theories of Jews writing during the eighteenth and nineteenth century have particular relevance to this chapter since Jews sought to show that Judaism, no less than Christianity, offered a universalistic theory of humanity and human dignity. Rather than chronicle the early writers, however, this bibliography refers to secondary sources that discuss their work from a modern perspective. Thus while Moses Mendelssohn and Gabriel Riesser are central exponents of a modern Jewish theory of human rights, the bibliography focuses on studies of their thought rather than on their original contributions. The one exception to this practice occurs in the case of Karl Marx. Marx is exceptional because he combines his original theory with a reflection on the social situation of Jews and their political demand for civil rights. He, therefore, provides both his own theory and a discussion of earlier theories in the light of modern Jewish political experience. That experience leads many contemporary Jews to develop theories of human rights so as to mobilize general support for specific Jewish causes — whether in response to the Nazi Holocaust, to problems in the State of Israel, or to the plight of Jews in the former Soviet Union.

Assuming that Judaism does indeed possess a theory of human rights, the next question becomes that of discovering what rights such a theory protects. The fourth chapter of the bibliography lists seventeen groups of rights and studies of how they have been construed under various theories of Jewish rights. These categories include general considerations such as the rights of the community, of women, and rights to freedom from racism. More specific rights such as those to movement, equality under the law, and freedom of movement also appear.

The fifth chapter looks at how modern Jewish history makes considerations of Jews and Judaism imperative in the study of human rights. The importance of Jews and Judaism is obvious in connection with three historical occurrences: the Nazi slaughter of six million Jews, the Soviet repression of Jewish culture, and the dilemmas facing the modern State of Israel. This chapter looks at specific cases in which Jews are purported to be victims of violations of human rights or violators of such rights.

Naturally, any single entry may have applicability to more than one chapter of the bibliography. A consideration of whether Judaism contains a theory of human rights often cites biblical and rabbinic precedent and then applies that precedent to modern concerns. The bibliography annotates such an entry in full, at its first appearance. The annotation summarizes the content of the entry and, thereby, anticipates its inclusion in later chapters. In those later chapters the annotation merely refers the reader to the original entry. Repeating an entry, although not its annotation, is necessary since some readers may wish to focus only on classical sources of Jewish theory, others on contemporary issues and applications, and still others may wish to concentrate primarily on questions of theory.

The three indexes provided are meant to guide readers in their use of the bibliography; access is to entry numbers, not page numbers. The author index refers to authors of the various entries rather than to authors mentioned in the annotations. Readers interested in the variety of writings by a single thinker will find this index useful. The title index also provides access to the enumerated citations. References are given for the title of each entry and for the anthologies and journals in which the entries appear. The third index is more general and concerns the basic subject matter in the annotations as well as the title of the entries. As a subject index it will not include reference to individuals who appear only once or twice in the bibliography. This subject index will not include the general categories which serve as basic rubrics in the bibliographical survey itself.

I have been helped in preparing this bibliography by the fine library staff at the University of Kansas, Watson Library, especially the Interlibrary Loan Services. The staff of the Asher Library of the Spertus College of Judaica in Chicago, Illinois, especially Dan Sharon, opened its stacks to me and helped me in my research. Colleagues have been exceedingly cooperative, especially through the medium of electronic mail. I should mention in particular Yosi Galron of Ohio State University and Bernard Jackson, Queen Victoria Professor of Law at the University of Liverpool, and editor of the *Jewish Law Annual*. My neighbor, friend, and colleague Dr. John Miller, Automation Librarian at the University of Kansas introduced me to at least some of the computer secrets necessary to generate this bibliography, and I am in his debt. As always The Reverend Dr. G. E. Gorman, advisor to the *Bibliographies and Indexes in Religious Studies* series and the entire Greenwood Press staff contributed to the improvement of this volume.

More personal interests also shaped this volume. My son's interests in Judaic studies and political philosophy have often overlapped with my own research for this bibliography. My daughter's study of Kurdish culture and nationalism has drawn my attention to questions of minority rights relevant for any investigation of human rights. Finally, the recent tragic and dramatic racial conflict in the United States gives witness to the need for more self-conscious study of human rights in both theory and practice. In one of the earliest systematic reflections on Judaism's theory of human rights, Moses Mendelssohn, over two hundred years ago, spoke of the need for education as a means of transforming society. He offered his philosophy of the relationship between the state and religion together with his theory of human rights in an effort to demonstrate the importance of ideas in transforming social life. He claimed that "There is only one infallible criterion for determining the quality of any form of government. It is the extent to which people are governed by means of education alone, so that government will be the product of moral standards and ethical convictions." This bibliography seeks to further that education which can lead to such a government.   It is dedicated to all those who share Mendelssohn's conviction.

Key Journals and
Periodical Sources

American Journal of Comparative Law
American Journal of International Law
Annuaire Francais de Droit International

Central Conference of American Rabbis Yearbook
Congress Monthly
Conservative Judaism

Dine Israel

Ethnic Studies Report

Harvard International Law Journal
Humanist
Human Rights Quarterly

Index on Censorship
International and Comparative Law Quarterly
International Yearbook on Human Rights
Israel Law Review
Israel Yearbook On Human Rights

Jewish Law Annual
Jewish Quarterly Review
Jewish Social Studies
Journal of Aging and Judaism
Journal of Halakha and Contemporary Society
Journal of Reform Judaism
Judaism

The Leo Baeck Institute Yearbook

Menorah Journal
Midstream
Modern Judaism

Political Theory
Proceedings of the Rabbinical Assembly

Reconstructionist
Revue des Droits de l'Homme. Human Rights Journal

Soviet Jewish Affairs
S'vara: A Journal of Philosophy and Judaism

Techumin: Torah, Society, and State: Compendium of Halakha
Tel Aviv University Law Review (Iyyunei Mishpat)
Tel Aviv University Studies in Law
Tradition

United Synagogue Review

Introductory Survey

DOES JUDAISM BELIEVE IN HUMAN RIGHTS?

Modern nationalism sometimes allows and encourages atrocities against groups within a particular nation. In response to such atrocities theorists often invoke the authority of rights that transcend even the sovereign independence of a nation. The problems stimulating the creation of such a theory arise from the peculiar status modernity gives to national sovereignty. The theory seeks to check excesses derived from the almost arbitrary power given to such states. While the development of a philosophic theory of universal human rights represents a peculiarly modern phenomenon, most theorists recognize its roots in earlier traditions (see entries 061, 065, 103, 111, 116, 125, 133, 223, 224, 296). These thinkers consider the tradition represented by the Hebrew Bible, if not by later Jewish thought, an important precedent on which a modern theory of human rights can rely. Nevertheless, a minority opinion, albeit an influential and significant one, rejects the Bible and Jewish thought generally as a source of the modern theory.

One influential view, advocated by thinkers such as Leo Strauss and Alasdair Macintyre, argues that the classical religious traditions lack a concept of inherent human rights (see entries 021, 135, 136, 260, 299). This argument contends that a religious tradition necessarily relies on revelation and divine authority. Rights and obligations flow from an act of the creator, not from the nature of human beings. Miracles reveal the contingency of all "natural" events. The will of the creator can relax both rights and obligations. Nature, therefore, provides no reliable or consistent guide to behavior.

Another view argues that Judaism does include a type of "natural law," but not a theory of "natural rights." This approach points to the stress on obligation rather than on privilege found in Jewish tradition (see entries 057, 140, 183, 247, 258, 278, 282, 283). From this perspective an emphasis on rights misconstrues the values a society must preserve. Society provides an environment enabling individuals to carry out their obligations. It is not a means of satisfying individual needs. At times the individual must defer such personal satisfaction for the sake of the common good. This argument means that an insistence on individual rights conflicts with the very purpose of social life. A theory of human rights not only misunderstands the meaning of human life but it also distorts the rationale for a social order.

Still another view, associated with Karl Marx, claims that religion merely reinforces the privileges of a certain class. When Jews, for example, clamor for human rights they merely ask for the privileges of bourgeois society. A true theory of human rights begins with the needs of humanity, conceived as an organic whole, not with particular individual desires. Only modernity holds the potential for either the conception of humanity required for a view of human rights or the implementation of that conception into a social program. From this perspective Judaism and Christianity share the limitations of class ideology (see entries 114, 190, 233, 262-297, 263, 270).

These various declarations that Judaism cannot possess a theory of human rights lead to some unfortunate consequences. Taken at face value they suggest that a bibliography such as the one presented here is ill advised. Any attempt to link Judaism and human rights misunderstands both Judaism and human rights. Several bibliographers on writings about human rights seem to accept this judgment, at least partially. These bibliographers do exclude consideration of Jews and Judaism, although they often do not exclude consideration of Christianity and Christian views of human rights (see entries 024, 025, 032, 044, 296). The error of accepting the negative assessment of Jewish involvement in human rights theory creates two problems. The first problem lies in the neglect of many important books and articles concerned with the theory of human rights. As the present bibliography shows, a wealth of literature written by and about Jews as a vehicle for reflections about human rights enriches the discussion about the theoretical and practical implications of the idea of human rights (as a useful contrast to the entries mentioned above see entry 024 which does include extensive coverage of Jewish interests in the theory of human rights). A second problem lies in the reduction of a very complex and often conflicting body of literature to only one position. Many scholars reject the judgment that the Hebrew Bible and Judaism possess no theory of human rights. Any single presentation of "the Jewish view" inevitably misrepresents the debate about this issue. Such a problem also arises in the case of anthologies devoted to "religion and human rights" which include, at best, only one essay focused on Judaism. While these essays often show the sensitivity and erudition of the author, even the most scrupulously honest writers inevitably skew the argument to fit their own position (note the generally fine, but clearly limited, contributions to entries 005, 018, 021).

Some theorists accept the general thesis that Judaism does not develop a view of human rights but then create their own theory which encompasses human rights under a slightly different rubric. Lenn E. Goodman, for example, evolves a theory of "desserts," or consequences which eschews the idea of rights, but does claim a correspondence between actions and consequences which underwrites a system very close to that found in a theory of rights (see entry 220). Michael Walzer also explicitly rejects a theory of rights, but offers an impressive system by which to ensure the protection of certain rights such as freedom, leisure, security, and welfare (see entries 138, 139). Merely because he rejects a general theory should not exclude his work from a consideration of the meaning of human rights.

Other writers argue that Judaism offers a dialectic between rights and duties. While not developing a single theory of universal human rights, the Hebrew Bible and rabbinic literature does safeguard certain possibilities of human life. The interaction between these safeguards and a willingness to suspend them if the need arises may complicate this theory but cannot negate the contribution it makes to any consideration of the idea of human rights (see entries 048, 059, 062, 073, 144). Human beings may indeed possess universal rights, even if they may not be inalienable under all circumstances.

A related argument suggests that specific implementations of Jewish law provide practical, if not theoretical, instruction in human rights. The Bible does not use the word "human rights." Nevertheless its laws do protect what many identify as such rights. It may not spell out a theory of the right to freedom; its regulation for the manumission of slaves shows that right in practice (see entries 062, 117). Stories of creation may attribute origins to a divine being, but also inculcate a theory of a predictable natural world in which the just regime is one that is hospitable to that nature (See entry 078). Rabbinical literature discusses the so-called Noahide laws, laws incumbent on all human beings. These laws effectively preserve the rights to property, to equality under law, and to life without enunciating a general theory of universal human rights (see entry 118). The particular rights protected in both biblical and rabbinic law deserve consideration when generating a general theory of human rights.

Theory often generalizes on the basis of practical experience. Jews, whose history in the modern world suggests the necessity to protect certain human freedoms, often evolve a theory of human rights on the basis of that historical experience. German Jews in the eighteenth century realized that only a theory of rights could protect their integration into the wider world of Western culture. Moses Mendelssohn and Gabriel Riesser articulated a Jewish theory of human rights both as a means of encouraging Jews to leave the protection of their particularism and as a way to persuade non-Jews that such integration was essential for any well functioning society. Studying the views on human rights advanced by the Jewish Enlightenment shows how theory and practice often interact and refine one another (see entries 152, 153, 154, 157, 160, 161, 179, 180, 279, 280, 294, 295).

In more recent times Jewish experience under both the Nazis and the Soviets led to reflection on human rights. Unwilling to ask for support merely because they are Jews, Jewish writers appeal to a general theory of human entitlement to mobilize world opinion. The Nazi holocaust, slaughtering six million Jews, one of the most traumatic events of the twentieth century, stimulated thinking about a theory of rights that might prevent such an atrocity from reoccurrence. Essays reflecting on Jewish suffering in the modern world become the foundation for demanding the protection of basic human rights (see entries 013, 016). The behavior of the Nazis suggests what occurs when one group of people deny the humanity of another group (see entries 111, 142). More contemporary events, however, suggest that antisemitism continues as a denial of basic rights to Jews. The experience of Jews in the former Soviet Union (entries 089, 161) stimulates a demand that people of good conscience work on behalf of all whose rights are curtailed. The problem of antisemitism among American blacks (entry 212) suggests that an advocacy of human rights may often disguise a plea for special self-interest. The very term used here, "antisemitism" reflects intellectual tensions and concerns. It really refers to actions directed against the Jews, not against "semites," of whom, of course, Jews are only one subgroup. When capitalized as "Anti-Semitism" the term implies the existence of some sort of entity called "Semitism." Some writers (see entry 212) indicate their discomfort with the term by using all lower case letters while retaining the hypen, thus, "anti-semitism." I prefer indicating that the word is a created one to refer to anti-Jewish actions or beliefs, thus when writing in my own words I will use "antisemitism," but retain the ambiguity demonstrated by the variety of usages in the literature.

This charge arises primarily in regard to the biased approach of the United Nations to human rights. According to the complaint, the United Nations condemns Israel for offenses against human rights while failing to condemn antisemitic actions of an even more extreme nature (see entries 014, 200, 371). Any advocacy for applying a theory of human rights should take into account both the possibility for abuse and unequal application of the theory and the possibility for self-serving interpretations of the theory. Studies of human rights theory in modern times should, at the very least, give attention to these complaints.

The experience of antisemitism despite the promises of equality led many Jews at the turn of the century to embrace Zionism. In so-doing several of these Jews enunciated their own understanding of human rights in contrast to the views of the German Jewish enlightenment. Whereas the German Jews focused on individual civil rights, the Eastern European Zionists focused on the right to national and cultural self-expression (see entries 168, 177, 222, 251, 252). Responding to the deprivation of cultural rights, these Jews insisted that all human communities enjoy natural rights to self-determination, the use of their native language, and to create its own social and civil structure. According to this view, the Enlightenment argument for civil rights missed the important point that these so-called "rights" were still granted as special privileges. Only the national sovereignty actualizes a natural right rather than depending upon an arbitrary gift.

From this standpoint the restoration of the Jewish national homeland should solve all questions of human rights. The actual history of the Jews in the land of Israel, however, points in a different direction. The conflict between Jew and non-Jewish Arab in Israel deeply divides loyalties within the state. In the search for peace some thinkers have evolved a theory of human rights that provides a criteria for action that transcends the "right to national sovereignty." Freedom of speech, equality before the law, freedom of movement, and even cultural rights are demanded for non-Jewish Arabs on the basis of a theory of human rights. In a self-consciously "Jewish" state the question of freedom of conscience naturally becomes important. A theory of human rights transcends the nation's cultural self-consciousness to require that all citizens participate in the right to freedom of religion. This theory applies equally to Jews, Muslims, Chinese, or Hindus. Several thinkers trace this transcendent theory back to Jewish sources (see entries 001, 002, 003, 012, 022, 109, 145, 146, 166, 167, 247, 267).

Many vocal elements within Israel claim that as a Jewish state it should be governed by religious, not secular, law. This contention evokes a response which demands a constitutional system that will guarantee human rights. The difficulties caused by the religious parties in Israel inspires many thinkers to call for the creation of a "bill of rights" to ensure that the state will not encroach on individual freedom (see entries 007, 056, 193, 204, 205, 286, 289). The very experience that Zionists thought would solve the problems of antisemitic attacks on Jewish rights had led to new problems. These problems in turn inspire reflection on a theory of human rights.

Jews confront modern problems beyond those associated with the State of Israel. As modern society wrestles with the rights demanded by women, racial minorities, and the poor, Jews look to their traditions for guidance. Two modern American Jewish theologians, Abraham Joshua Heschel (see entries 087-094, 228) and Mordecai M. Kaplan (see entries 097, 098, 235, 237), respond to these problems by articulating theories of human rights based on Jewish sources and couched in modern Western terms. Not only these thinkers but several others examine contemporary social issues from the perspective of Jewish thinking. They often express themselves in terms drawn from the language of human rights theory. Thus an analysis of the status of women in Judaism may draw on the language of human rights to suggest introducing changes into Jewish law (see entries 054, 122). The differences dividing various Jewish leaders in response to the modern situation often depend on the way they see a modern theory of human rights interacting with modern experience in their own lives and in the lives of their followers (see entry 172).

Several authors included in the first three chapters of this bibliography offer their own theories of human rights as drawn from the sources of Judaism. A later chapter focuses on specific theories. It is clear, however, that ignoring the body of literature written by and about Jews in connection with a theory of human rights neglects important perspectives on that theory. Even if one agrees with the negative judgment that a system of revealed truth cannot develop a consistent theory of natural rights, the reflections by those who disagree require analysis and consideration. The very bulk of the material makes their omission serious; the variety of issues studied makes their content of inherent interest. Does Judaism believe in human rights? That question demands further investigation. Jews, however, do indeed declare such a belief and have described it in detail. Jews and Jewish experience, moreover, have been catalysts for generating theories about human rights. Whatever Judaism may or may not believe about the nature of human obligation, about the theoretical rights appertaining to individuals, or the specific rights classical Jewish sources protect or ignore, serious study of the theory of human rights must acknowledge Jewish involvement as theorists, as victims of abuse or as perpetrators of such abuse.

HUMAN RIGHTS IN THE BIBLE AND TALMUD

Several arguments claim that the Bible and Talmud, the classical sources of Jewish thought, contain no theory of universal human rights. The Bible certainly contains injunctions concerning interhuman behavior — the Ten Commandments, the laws in Exodus, Leviticus, and Deuteronomy all emphasize humanistic concerns. The legal material of the Talmud and its development in later rabbinic thinking provides valuable instruction concerning the protection of life, property, and personal freedom. Nevertheless, theorists of human rights sometimes claim that the very context of these legal concerns — a divinely revealed code — prevent the development of a genuinely universalist theory of human rights. One argument (see entries 044, 135, 136, 141) contends that only philosophy can generate a theory of natural rights possessed by every human person.

Revelation, on this reading, only offers a series of privileges granted to creatures by a sovereign creator. All so-called "rights" are, in fact, only gifts granted by arbitrary will to those whom God favors. The divine discretion can grant more privileges to one group of human beings and fewer to others. No human being enjoys absolute and irrevocable rights merely by virtue of being human. One facet of this argument, then, derives from the arbitrary nature of whatever "rights" people may be granted. A second aspect of this argument derives from the expectations on individuals or communities to grant rights to others. A genuine philosophical theory of rights assumes human autonomy. Human beings have the moral freedom to choose how they behave toward one another. A religious theory, however, assumes that ultimate control lies in the hands of the divinity. Because history, if not individual human destiny, depends on the divine will, the construction of society remains outside human control. While humanity may earn merit or demerit by its actions, it does not hold its future in its own hands. Neither the individual nor society bears ultimate responsibility for the shape of history.

While this argument claims that only a humanistic philosophy can generate a viable theory of human rights, a related position focuses on the social and political consequences of religious ideology (see entries 114, 115, 139). The Bible and Talmud reflect the particularistic interests of a certain community. More specifically, these texts articulate the social vision of the leadership within that community. Rather than expressing a broadly human conception of rights, these texts reinforce the narrow self-interests of a small elite. Some critics use this particularism to reject the Bible and Talmud as authentic sources for a theory of human rights (see entry 114); others (139) accept such self-interest as an inherent part of any human thinking and take particularism as a point of departure and eschew the very concept of a universalistic philosophy of human rights. At the very least such thinkers refuse to take these texts *in their totality* as a basis for a theory of human rights. While much in the Bible and Talmud may inspire people to altruistic action and consideration of others, much within those texts serves chauvinistic concerns. The biblical charge to exterminate the Amalekites, for example, must temper too positive an evaluation of the Bible as a modern resource. Despite offering valuable lessons in non-violence, the Bible, given such examples of particularistic fervor, cannot be said to offer a consistent theory of universal rights (see entry 115).

These arguments suggest that religious texts taken at face value do not provide an unambiguous theory of universal human rights. Some defenders of the relevance of the Bible and Talmud as well-springs of thinking about human rights agree with the general point expressed. Indeed, the Bible and Talmud are not yet theories of universal human rights. They do, however, show how a community gradually concretizes the ideals and values that provide the necessary foundation for such a theory. The Bible and Talmud, on this reading, insist on certain general principles such as love of neighbor and the dignity of humanity upon which any concept of universal human rights depends (see entries 041, 047, 051, 061, 062, 065, 073, 075, 076, 080, 086, 088, 092, 093, 096, 097, 104, 105, 111, 116-119, 125-127, 130, 144, 145). This view rests on two presuppositions. The first claims that a theory of human rights needs more than either empirical data or philosophical reflection alone provide. Human rights need grounding in a transcendent source. Only such a basis for these rights gives them the power to override political and pragmatic considerations. Religious texts such as the Bible and Talmud root personal and social rights in the will of a transcendent divinity. While such a claim may appear arbitrary and sometimes appears in the context of an exclusivism and particularism, it also renders rights inalienable and indisputable. Despite the disadvantages in a religious foundation for a theory of rights expressed by the critics, these defenders of the Talmud and Bible emphasize that without reference to the divine, human rights depend on the far more arbitrary will of human communities.

Perhaps the most dramatic example of such a claim occurs in Genesis 19, the story of Sodom and Gomorrah (see entry 126). The Sodomites infringe on a universal human right — that to protection and hospitality. Because of that they are punished by God. The divine sanction provides the basis for enforcing the laws of hospitality which apply in any place and to any person. Certainly the Sodomites could argue on pragmatic and social grounds that they have sovereignty over their own territory. Indeed, they reject the appeal of Lot that they moderate their demands because he is a "stranger" among them. The universal relevance of the claim to hospitality is symbolized in the story not through social or pragmatic considerations but by the introduction of the divine.

A second part of this argument claims that historical conditions shape the actual practice of any human community. Thus the very real limitations found in the codes of the Bible and Talmud merely reflect the contexts in which they appeared. The biblical prophets, for example, recognized this element in their own tradition (see entries 041, 074, 075, 081, 109, 146). They continually recalled their communities to the ideals and values which should animate their social programs. That these programs often fell short of the ideal goals of the community itself actually shows that the Bible or Talmud cannot be rejected on the basis of its practical achievements. These achievements, as the prophets recognize, do not fully represent the vision of the nation itself. Thus the incomplete realization of the ideal of universal human rights in biblical and talmudic texts does not disqualify those texts from consideration as the grounds of a theory of human rights. The tensions within these traditions shows that equality and human freedoms were ideals and goals, as values toward which society strived (see entry 120) and hence relevant for any modern consideration of those values and goals. The mechanism of the levirate marriage, for example (entry 042), may no longer serve the needs of a modern society. Even the rabbinic modification of those laws do not protect either a woman's private rights or the more general right to create a family. Nevertheless, the advance from the primitive biblical legislation through later rabbinic revisions of it show how the principle of both family rights and women's rights finds different expression according to the historical context. The modern world may need to alter these early laws drastically. These prototypical laws, however, illuminate basic concerns that should animate modern thinking.

A different argument transforms what appears as a liability into a basis for affirming the relevance of Jewish texts to a consideration of human rights. These texts emphasize the importance of lawfulness, of social legislation, of ensuring the welfare of individuals by means of communal regulations. This judicial perspective challenges modern societies as they seek to establish means for protecting the welfare of their citizens. In this way the legalism of the Bible and Talmud, its concern with duties rather than with rights, teaches an important lesson necessary when deriving a theory of human rights (see entries 043, 048, 050, 056, 057, 069, 077, 078, 079, 085, 116, 124, 133). The classical texts of Judaism draw attention to the importance of providing safeguards to balance the demands of the community against the needs of the individual. Whether or not the Bible or Talmud anticipates modern theories of rights, it does anticipate the call for a legal system that officially recognizes the limits beyond which either individuals or the community as a social entity can encroach on the privileges of others.

Here again, the religious content appears as an advantage not a liability. The Bible and Talmud do not cast the question as that of the individual against society but as subjective desire against the objective will of the divine (see entry 043). Society needs to enact certain laws and the individual needs to follow certain regulations not merely for private reasons, but because the divine will structures reality in a certain way (see entry 057). Appeal to a transcendent divine creator underwrites a democratic legal system because it attributes an equal right to all creatures. Laws must ensure a right to representation because despite their inherent differences all individuals play an important role in a plan which humanity can only dimly perceive (see entries 058, 075). This emphasis appears to some thinkers (see entries 076, 077) a distinctly Jewish contribution to the idea of human rights in contrast to a Christian reliance on grace and the goodness of a reformed human nature.

A final attempt to refute the claim that Jewish sources do not recognize a theory of universal human rights musters specific examples of how those sources protect certain rights. Several biblical and talmudic injunctions protect "the right to life" particularly in the case of the terminally ill (see entries 045, 046, 053, 063, 123, 127, 128-132). Family rights also constitute an important topic in biblical and rabbinic writings whether in regard to the rights of women or in relationship to questions of birth, birth control, and abortion (see entries 054, 067, 110, 122, 402). These primary texts also evince great concern for freedom of conscience and toleration of those with dissenting views (see entries 081, 082, 087, 089, 095, 109, 140, 143-145). Scholars also find within those works references to various social rights including those to medical care, to personal welfare — whether psychological or physiological, to privacy, to freedom of expression, the right to dissent, and to peace from violence, in several classical texts (see entries 056, 064, 066, 070, 073, 090, 091, 094, 100, 101, 128, 138, 139). Finally, the Bible and Talmud yield principles that ensure equity before the law, and the protection of the legal rights of all citizens (see entries 049, 050, 052, 083, 108, 113). While not necessarily implying a theory about human rights, each of these sets of concerns demonstrates how the texts Jews hold sacred do indeed protect those concerns usually associated with human rights.

JEWISH THEORIES OF HUMAN RIGHTS

In light of the conflicting views about whether Judaism has a theory of human rights and the disputed evidence for such a theory in the classic sources of Judaism, the variety of Jewish theories of human rights comes as no surprise. Scholars note the tensions and ambiguities within Jewish thinking that make the isolation of a single theory of human rights exceedingly difficult (see entries 149, 150, 162, 171, 180, 302, 303). This consideration leads some thinkers like Eugene B. Borowitz (see entries 178-181) and Jacob Agus (see entries 150-151) to emphasize a dialectic between the various strands within Jewish thinking.

Among those strands two derive from a self-consciously theological perspective. According to one perspective human rights flow from the infinite worth of the individual human being derived from the divine image invested in each person. The sacredness of each human being depends, in this instance, on the resemblance between the creator and the creature. The inalienable right to life depends on this correspondence between the human and the divine. The Jewish theory of human rights, from this perspective, serves as a counterpoint to the normative western theory which begins with natural rights. The contribution that the Jewish view makes appears most prominently in the works of Abraham Joshua Heschel (see entries 226-229) which take seriously the divine image within each person. On the basis of that idea, Heschel advocates social changes that will ensure rights to every person. Other traditional Jewish thinkers also urge the enforcement of rights on the basis of each human being's sacred status (see entries 157, 159, 165, 171, 199, 210, 213, 215, 220, 225, 236, 245, 248, 250, 272, 275, 278, 290).

A second theological strand emphasizes the duties that God places on human beings. Humanity serves a divine purpose; it fulfills its destiny only if it furthers that greater goal. This emphasis on duties includes an awareness that rights accompany expectations. People can perform their expected tasks only if society enables them to fulfill their potential. Human dignity consists in the ability each person has to help realize God's intention for the world. Society, however, can thwart that ability, and God's plan succeeds only when laws reinforce the divine project which lies at the heart of human dignity. This view, like the preceding one, often criticizes normative western theory. It, too, considers divine empowerment, not natural rights, the basis for enacting legislation to protect each person's opportunity to contribute to history (see entries 157, 162, 173-176, 185, 198, 202, 204, 209, 218, 224, 241, 242, 247, 258, 269, 281, 282, 283, 292, 308, 309).

This emphasis on duties rather than rights often produces a stress on the needs of the community rather than those of the individual. At the least it recognizes a standard outside that of the individual's own needs as the basis for granting rights to a person. In reaction to this view several thinkers claim that Jewish thought does protect the individual as such. According to this view, Judaism grants rights to individuals in their own right rather than merely respecting them as a players in a divine game. The rights of the individual, Louis Rabinowitz claims in response to Aharon Lichtenstein, derive directly from each person's responsibility before God (see entries 204, 258 and 274). While Chaim Reines (see entry 278) criticizes the individualism espoused by the Jewish philosopher Hermann Cohen, the psychologist Reuven Bulka defends individualism from a traditional Jewish standpoint (see entry 187). Amnon Carmi (see entry 191) explores the idea of personal freedom as a foundational concept in any theory of human rights and in Jewish thought generally.

The debate between those who rest a theory of human rights on individual freedom and those who focus on duties and communal responsibility reflects the predicament of Jews in the modern world. Rather than arising from the texts of classical Judaism, the problems confronting Jews today derive from life experience. Jews today face a pluralistic world. The various theories of human rights generalize from Jewish particularism to create a theory appropriate for the modern world. Abraham Beame discovers liberalism in Judaism because he seeks a theory within Judaism relevant for the modern context (see entry 163). That essay suggests some problems found in the labels used to designate thinkers. Political alliances to "liberal" or "conservative" factions do not translate automatically into religious liberalism or conservatism. Used here the terms refer to how a thinker views Jewish tradition. A "liberal" sees that tradition as a resource for the individual, as a means by which individuals actualize and use their potential. For liberals the good of the individual acts as a limit upon the rights of the tradition to dictate behavior. A "conservative" claims that the tradition restricts the options of the individual. Individual "rights" are measured by their approximation of traditional rules and regulations. If the language of rights reinforces tradition, then that language is legitimated. If the language of rights impairs an ability to fulfill traditional obligations, then the language must be sacrificed. The terms "liberal" and "conservative" used in this survey refer to these two alternative approaches.

The significance of this difference appears most clearly as modern Jews struggle to make sense of their particularistic tradition for lives lived in a pluralistic setting. American and Israeli scholars debate the meaning of human rights as they seek ways to live in a pluralistic environment (see entry 172). Louis Henkin (see entry 224) recognizes Jewish discontent with the modern response to the question of human rights but urges an understanding of the social and historical context in which this response occurs.

The history of Jewish experience with non-Jews makes such understanding difficult. Indeed, one non-theological strand in Jewish thinking about human rights arises from that historical experience. Jews have felt the sting of persecution and evolved a theory of human rights to express their outrage not only as victims of persecution but as defenders of a universalistic view of humanity. Leo Strauss (see entry 301) constructed his philosophical system with full awareness of the dangers present in both secularism and religious fanaticism. Other thinkers raise this awareness to a major principle: human rights consist primarily in the right of individuals and groups to exist despite their difference from others. The treatment of Jews in the former Soviet Union (see entries 161, 195, 231, 302) suggests that society needs to enact a non-discrimination principle that applies to all minorities. Jewish experience under the Nazis awakens a realization that when any part of society suffers the entire society feels the pain. Antisemitism, whether in Germany or in the United States stimulates recognition of this interaction between a society's treatment of its minorities and its own ability to survive. This experience becomes another principle on which to build a theory of human rights (see entries 194, 212, 231, 255) Here a human rights theory grows out of life rather than out of theology or theoretical abstractions.

This type of theorizing typifies modern Jewish theories of human rights. Some thinkers, as noted above, locate a theory of human rights in the classical sources of Judaism; others dispute this claim. No one, however, doubts that eighteenth and nineteenth century Jewish thinkers developed theories of human rights that they associated with Judaism. Thinkers such as Moses Mendelssohn and Leopold Zunz presented a broad conception of universal rights as the basis for admitting Jews into general civil society. Against this position of the Jewish Enlightenment, non-Jews argued that citizens must earn their rights. Only when Jews prove worthy of being accepted in society will society open its arms to them. This debate forced Jews to defend themselves and their tradition. Jews, they argued, never sought to separate from the general world in which they lived. They had been unfairly excluded from that society, but they had not chosen such exclusion willingly. These Jews argued that society as a whole benefits by expanding to include divergent communities. Jews, they argued, possess an intense social consciousness, a concern for the welfare of the polity, and respect for law and order. Including such citizens within a state would strengthen its inner life and add to its economic prosperity. A nation that protects the human rights of its citizens is more able to survive than a nation which revokes those rights in a misguided sense of self-interest. The theories and arguments offered by Jews in the Enlightenment reflect their historical context more than they reflect the classical sources of Judaism. Nevertheless they need to be considered as evidence of Jewish theories concerning universal human rights (see entries 150, 152, 259, 260, 273, 279, 280, 294, 295). In this theory human rights consist of civil liberties and the right to participate fully in social life.

One of the most important theories concerning human rights, that of Karl Marx, cannot be understood except in the context of this debate about the Jews and human rights (see entries 262, 263, 270, 271). Marx contends that Jews have misunderstood their own predicament. They think that what they lack is civil status. In fact what they lack is a truly human society. The position of the Jews, Marx thinks, reveals the sorry state of humanity in the modern world. Only by curing the alienation that afflicts everyone can the Jews find their own cure. When society cures itself, then the language of rights will no longer be needed (see entry 153). Scholars debate whether Marx sympathized with the plight of the Jew or not (see entries 154, 156, 190, 201, 216, 279, 287, 291). His view on the mistaken concern for civil rights as a means of protecting human rights generally offers an important contribution to human rights theory. Marx roots his theory in an understanding of human society, not in a claim to natural rights.

Jewish thinkers other than Karl Marx rejected the theories of the Jewish Enlightenment. Eastern European Zionists, like Marx, claimed that civil rights were a poor substitute for human rights. From their perspective true human existence depends on having an independent and recognizable culture. From this perspective the basic human right is not that of an individual but of a cultural community. Jews who demand human rights should be seeking the rights to self-determination, to their native language, and to the practice of their particularistic customs (see entries 170, 177, 222, 234, 251). Zionists did not deny that individuals have rights and duties. They did deny the possibility of actualizing individual potential without an independent social and cultural context in which such actualizing could take place. Here cultural autonomy represents the most basic human right since without it no individual life, much less individual rights, can be possible. Zionists created a Jewish state in an attempt to ensure the protection of this most basic right and to build on its foundation a national life designed to protect individual rights as well.

In practice the creation of the independent State of Israel brought with it more problems than it solved. The meaning of human rights takes on a different meaning when the question is no longer that of protecting one's own rights but of determining the rights of others. The modern State of Israel understands itself as a democratic nation in which Jews and non-Jews enjoy the same rights of citizenship. Nevertheless, Israelis find it hard to agree on what rights they can allow to dissident groups within their borders, what rights of personal conscience they can allow to Jews who refuse to follow traditional Jewish law, and what rights to judicial procedure can be deferred on the grounds of religious and national requirements (see entries 166, 167, 170, 172, 193, 214, 230). Do human beings possess a right to freedom from religion? This question underlies many discussions of "human rights" in the State of Israel. A theory of human rights that does not include freedom from religion but only freedom *for* one or another religion seems to some Israeli thinkers inadequate; the religious leaders in Israel disagree (see entries 182, 264, 286, 291). The experience of Jews in their own land, no less than their experience as victims in other countries, raise questions about what should or should not be included in a theory of human rights.

JUDAISM AND SPECIFIC HUMAN RIGHTS

The differences between specific Jewish theories of human rights influence Jewish thinkers in identifying and describing particular rights. The selection of rights discussed often depends on contextual factors; as one or another social or personal issue commands general attention, Jews analyze it from the perspective of a particular theory of human rights. The section of the bibliographical survey devoted to "specific human rights" shows how general theory shapes analysis of particular issues. Despite applying theories to different cases, the analysis falls into five general categories: that of preserving the sacred image of humanity, of cultivating a sense of duty in fulfilling divinely given obligations, of responding to the social problems exposed symptomatically by antisemitism, of adapting to a pluralistic world setting, and of coping with the demands arising from an independent Jewish state and its political dilemmas.

Several Zionists emphasize the community's rights to self-determination and cultural expression (see entries 313, 315, 317). Their argument gains support from those who root such rights in the Jewish experience as a persecuted minority and who derive from that experience a general principle granting all minorities comparable rights (see entries 311, 318; compare entries under the rubric "Minorities" and under the rubric "Movement"). In contrast, some thinkers emphasize the rights of the community as a necessary check on individualism (see entry 312) or as an expression of democratic principles (see entry 314).

The right to freedom of conscience finds its most dramatic discussion in relationship to religious legislation passed in the modern State of Israel (see entries 320, 321, 323, 324, 326-329, 333-335, 337). More general studies look at the right of conscience as an expression of individualism (see entries 319, 331, 337). A contrasting view emphasizes that responsibility for the community and duties to God limit even an individual's freedom of conscience (see entries 331, 336).

Consideration of conscience leads naturally into a discussion of the right to dissent from public policy, most prominently the right to dissent from participation in a war legally declared within a particular nation. Here again some entries focus on the rights of the individual (see entries 338, 340, 347), while others limit that right in view of the duties owed to society (see entries 345, 346). Debate about the justification of war divides in a similar way with conservatives granting society the right to declare war (see entries 510, 513, 514) and liberals focusing on the individual's right to dissent from the social consensus (see entries 511, 512).

The German Jewish Enlightenment stressed the right to equality as the central freedom natural to every human being. Enlightenment Jews such as Moses Mendelssohn constructed their arguments for emancipating the Jews on the basis of this putative right. Naturally opponents of the Enlightenment suggest the limitations of such an analysis of the Jewish condition (see entries 348, 353, 356, 360, 370, 375, 379, 380, 384). The modern experience of persecution, particularly in the former Soviet Union and under the Nazis, underlies many contemporary Jewish affirmations of this right (see entries 349, 368, 371, 382). In an ironic reversal, Israeli treatment of the non-Jewish Arab population also stimulates reflection on the human right to equality as a Judaic principle (see entries 351, 352, 355, 357, 362). Several entries respond to modern conditions indirectly by offering interpretations of classical Jewish texts that seem to illuminate the meaning of equality in the modern period (see entries 350, 354, 358, 359, 361, 365, 372, 374, 377, 378, 383). Some entries focus on particular contemporary issues regarding the equality of persons such as racial and gender discrimination (see entries 364, 366, 373). Still other entries suggest a more general theory of equality which, while not necessarily citing Jewish sources, reveals sensitivity to the inner dynamic in the Judaic tradition (see entries 362, 383).

The right to freedom of expression finds ardent defenders who see it as essential to individual freedom (see entries 387, 389, 390) but also advocates arguing that the communal good requires individuals to limit their freedom for the general welfare (see entries 391, 393, 394). Political policies of the Israeli state arouse considerable discussion. Some writers note the comparative freedom of expression in that country in contrast to that enjoyed in other nations under siege (see entries 385, 386). The alternative argument that Israel suffers from censorship also finds expression (see entries 388, 394).

Discussion of family rights in Jewish thought divides between those who emphasize duties that restrict individual freedom (see entries 396, 397, 399, 400, 402) and those who advocate individual rights even at the expense of social concerns (see entries 395, 397, 401). A similar dichotomy separates those who claim the supreme value of personal freedom (see entries 405, 406) and those who argue the need to limit that freedom (see entries 403, 404). In contrast, all the entries concerning the right to health (see entries 407-413) recognize the importance of balancing personal and social concerns in regard to satisfying medical needs.

A clear division between liberal and conservative thinkers appears in regard to the right to work. What rights does the laborer enjoy in relation to the employer? Those emphasizing Judaism as a system of duties focus on the balance needed between respect for the rights of the worker and the rights of the employer (see entries 414, 416, 419, 420). Liberals tend to stress the importance of creating a viable environment for labor. Such an environment includes the preservation of such rights as those to health compensation, to strike and to have free time (see entries 415, 417, 421).

Three considerations govern discussions about human rights in relation to the legal system. One set of concerns arise around the process of law itself. A general consensus agrees that Jewish tradition emphasizes an equality in judicial review for Jew and non-Jew, for minority and majority community alike (see entries 422, 424, 425, 427, 429, 430, 432, 439, 440, 446, 447, 450, 451, 453). A second set of issues arise from the practice of law in the modern State of Israel. Some concerns arise from the treatment of minority groups (see entries 423, 426, 431, 437, 444). Other questions focus on the legal status of rights in a nation governed by religious precedent; several writers claim that only a written constitution can guarantee equality before the law (see entries 435, 436, 440, 443, 454). The proponents of individual dignity oppose the advocates of a theory of duties most clearly over the third judicial issue — that of appropriate forms of punishment. A theory based on "desserts" often defends extreme types of punishment as necessary for the social order (see entries 428, 438, 445, 447). A theory emphasizing the inalienable dignity of every individual often opposes punishments that seem excessive (see entries 433, 455).

The division between individualists and duty-oriented theorists becomes obvious in the discussion of the "right to life" and the "right to die." Those who stress individual dignity advocate each person's right to decide whether to live or die (see entries 457, 465-467, 470, 471, 482, 487). The preponderant view, however, suggests that duty requires the preservation of life. A similar division occurs in regard to the "right to privacy." Liberals defend this right as protected by the Jewish commitment to individualism (see entries 500-502), while conservatives generally hedge the right with duties to the community (see entries 498, 499, 503-505). In the same way, conservatives suggest the limits to a society's responsibility to ameliorate the condition of the poor (see entry 521), while liberals (who in this case predominate) argue for pervasive mechanisms to protect the dignity and welfare of the poor (see entries 515, 516, 517, 522).

Divisions concerning the right to non-discrimination on the basis of race depend on whether an author turns to Jewish sources as a means of understanding modern problems like Abraham Joshua Heschel (see entries 508, 509) or looks at the actual interaction of Jews and American blacks (see entries 506, 507). The different views on the rights of women according to Judaism divide between those who rely on classical texts and those who take their cue from modern events. The former draw on a religious perspective that defines the social roles of men no less than women. The latter (see entries 523-537) use the language of human rights to advocate granting equality to women in every sphere of human activity, even when recognizing traditional teachings to the contrary.

HUMAN RIGHTS AND CONTEMPORARY JUDAISM

Several of the issues raised previously arise as much from Jewish experience as from the classical sources of Judaism. This historical experience has relevance not merely for Jews seeking to understand the meaning of human rights but for a more general quest to comprehend the basis on which to theorize the existence of such universal values. The struggles within the modern State of Israel to cope with secularism and its expectations adumbrate a tension within modern society generally (see entries 538, 544, 548, 550, 552, 554, 555, 557, 560, 568, 572, 573, 574, 578, 580, 581, 582, 584, 586-590, 596-599, 601, 605, 620, 623, 631, 647, 648, 653, 661, 671, 675, 677, 682, 692, 696, 707-710, 713-717, 720, 725, 728, 729, 733-736, 745, 746, 747, 751). While as a self-consciously "Jewish" state Israel may face the problems of reconciling personal conscience with social self-understanding in an acute fashion, every society envisions itself according to certain ideals and values. The rights of the individual need to be balanced against the ability of the communal body to maintain a consistent ideology and corporate selfhood. Israel strives to balance the rights to freedom of religion for the traditional Jews in its borders with the rights to freedom from religion for non-Jews and non-religious Jews. The specifically Jewish nature of the laws involved point beyond themselves to the more general question of freedom of conscience generally. In the same way Israel's necessity of coping with a hostile internal threat from some of its own citizens (notably the non-Jewish Arab population) raises more general problems. One question asks how a community's self-perceived danger authorizes infringement on individual rights. The response of Arab countries generally to the existence of the Jewish state arouses concern as well. The persecution of Jews in Arab countries as a consequence of hostility to Israel represents a parallel to the problems of Arab Muslims in Israel (see entries 573, 636). Jewish writers often point to a related concern. Commissions of the United Nations appear to evaluate human rights abuses differently for political rather than philosophical reasons. Persecutions against Jews are ignored; problems within the State of Israel are exaggerated. Several Jewish thinkers suggest that this phenomenon undermines the theory of human rights. If the theory can be abused for political self-interest it may prove useless as a principle for improving the world situation (see entries 544, 558, 569, 579, 602, 603, 606, 634, 639, 648, 651, 661,665, 666, 676, 679, 691, 692, 741).

This analysis of the actions of the United Nations symbolizes a common process in Jewish writings about human rights. The Jewish case becomes symptomatic of more general issues. Both the leaders of the Jewish Enlightenment and their critics, with Marx as the foremost one, interpreted the Jewish quest for rights as paradigmatic. How society treats Jews, they argued, shows its strengths and weaknesses (see entries 542, 545, 546, 549, 562, 604, 632, 633, 663, 672, 673, 669, 681, 689, 694, 698, 699, 711, 730, 731, 742). Even Zionists generalized from the problematics of Jewish life to a theory about minority rights generally (see entries 553, 562, 595, 616, 742). The most prominent example of such thinking occurs in relation to Jewish experience under the Nazis. While Jews were not the only victims of the Nazi attempt to purify their race, they have become emblematic of that attempt. The slaughter of six million Jews, the holocaust of European Jewry, signifies both the atrocities that human beings can perpetrate on one another and the necessity for legal structures to prevent such atrocities. Jews and non-Jews alike examine the Nazi case and seek to evoke from it general principles that will eliminate genocide as a viable political program in the future (see entries 543, 558, 594, 600, 664, 670, 705, 715, 728). In contemporary history the plight of the Jews in the former Soviet Union plays a similar role. Theorists have used that situation to indicate the necessity for securing certain human rights more firmly (see entries 560, 577, 583, 585, 626, 627, 634, 635, 637, 638, 650, 666, 667, 685, 706, 728, 740, 741). In this way the inability of Soviet Jews to emigrate to Israel illuminated the need to secure rights to free movement; abolition of Jewish worship suggests the importance of the right to freedom of conscience; elimination of Yiddish culture argues for a group's right to its own culture. The new problems created by the break-up of the Soviet Union bring equally poignant questions to the fore, discussion of which, however, have appeared too recently to be included in this bibliography.

A final way in which Jewish experience becomes a point of departure for reflection on human rights derives from the Jewish involvement in modernity. From the eighteenth century onward Jews embraced the new secular world of rationalism that emerged from the religiously dominated pre-modern society. On the one hand the acceptance of modernity meant that many Jews sought to modify their own tradition where it seemed to conflict with the new values. Perhaps the most obvious example of such modification occurs in the sphere of women's rights (see entries 646, 653, 659, 687, 697, 718). What once appeared an acceptable definition of gender roles became under the impact of experience no longer viable. The equality granted women usually came as a protest against rather than as an application of traditional religious values. Other responses to modernity were less positive. Jews discovered the liabilities of modernity no less than its advantages. The discrepancies between the rights promised them and the experiences modern society afforded them led many Jews to question and revise the original theories of human rights and equality that they had accepted. The American-Jewish community illustrates this reconsideration of theory in the light of practical life experience (see entries 551, 591, 593, 606, 717, 643, 661, 668, 674, 692, 722, 728). The impact of black antisemitism causes many Jews to wonder whether the general theory of universal rights actually benefits society as a whole. Jews and blacks often mean different things by terms such as human rights and equality and they disagree over whether such programs as affirmative action fall under those terms (see entries 547, 576, 621, 690, 743).

CONCLUSIONS

Several sections of the bibliographical survey include selections that question whether the Jewish tradition supports a philosophical theory of universal human rights. Readers will, of course, come to their own conclusions. The definitive impact of history rather than doctrine, however, suggests that Jewish thought as classically understood had neither the motivation nor the resources for creating such a theory. Nevertheless, as the same sections of the bibliographical survey testify, astute interpreters of Judaism today do generate such a theory out of the texts of the Jewish tradition. At the very least most Jewish thinkers argue *for the relevance* of their tradition for reflecting on any theory of human rights. This consensus suggests certain conclusions.

The first conclusion is theological. A modern theology loses credibility if the God it envisions does not protect and value the rights of every human being. Sometimes that theology portrays God as protector of those rights through a system of duties incumbent on all people; sometimes the idea of God serves as the basis on which theorists postulate the very existence of such rights. This survey shows how various Jewish thinkers justify their theological claims by reference to a system of rights and a legal securing of them. A second point emerges as well. Theology often presents itself as the *only* basis from which to argue for universal rights. Not only do several writers argue that a God-idea functions to support a theory of human rights. They also argue that without a grounding in a transcendent value a theory of universal rights cannot stand.

A second conclusion can be called "anthropological," that is, it deals with the nature of humanity. A theory of human rights based on the assumption of individual liberty entails a different set of expectations than one based on the assumption of individual responsibility. Whether a theory construes human nature as inherently separatist and individualistic or as social and bound to society shapes the particular rights affirmed and protected. A choice concerning a theory of humanity shapes specific decisions concerning such diverse rights as those for freedom of conscience, dissent from public policy, equality of treatment, freedom of expression, health and medical treatment, freedom from discrimination, to work, and the rights of women. The patterns found in the bibliographical theory dividing traditionalists and non-traditionalists supports the intuition that theories of human rights depend on a prior theory about human nature.

The necessity for repetition of entries in the bibliographical survey points in a third direction. Decisions about specific human rights and about a general theory of human rights intertwine. A general theory reveals its implications when applied to specific cases. Specific cases gain persuasiveness when placed in the context of a general theory. In a more sociological vein, a society creates its self-image through a combination of specific actions and a comprehensive ideal identity. A theory of human rights defines a community's ideals and self-perception. Within the framework of those values, however, members disagree about the relative significance of specific concerns. Nevertheless an accumulation of dissenting concerns transforms the very framework that creates the community. Again, while changing a particular theory may not necessarily alter attitudes toward a specific issue in human rights, such a change may indicate a transformed self-image. The relationship between any tradition and its theory of human rights depends on both the general self-perception the tradition holds and on the specific instances of that self-perception exemplified in specific legal cases.

The final point is perhaps the most important one: a theory of human rights depends as much on its historical realism as on its philosophical rigor. Jewish victimization in recent history and the dilemmas associated with the politics of the modern State of Israel constitute decisive facts with which any theory must grapple. Jewish reflection on the theory of universal human rights injects an essential note of suspicion into the discussion. The political uses made of that theory renders any particular advocacy of it suspect. Jewish defenders of the idea from the Enlightenment to the present have served their perceived self-interest. Non-Jews who invoke the theory as a form of modern antisemitism also exhibit their prejudices and narrow interests. Women who rely on modernity to ensure their rights and black Americans who turn to human rights theory to criticize Jewish Americans represent only one response to contemporary life. Other responses include that of Jews who reject the language of rights in favor of duty and of Marxists who reject it as a misunderstanding of historical process.

The annotated bibliographical survey that follows offers a critical selection of the material that supports the four conclusions just noted. Readers should study that material carefully. They will, perhaps, discover conclusions of their own, challenge the ones presented here, or modify the summary analysis given above. Such study serves at least two purposes. Readers will confront the variety of Jewish reflections on the theory of human rights and its application. They will also confront the possibility that the theory suffers from severe, even fatal, flaws and cannot function as its proponents hope. Readers, after using this bibliographical survey, will make their own decisions and draw their own conclusions. This work invites them to join a continuing discussion and offers them an opportunity to begin the process of decision making.

Bibliographical Survey

1

General Works
and Anthologies

ANTHOLOGIES

001   "Symposium on Human Rights: Groups (Minority) Rights." *Israel Yearbook on Human Rights* 1 (1971): 393-418.

> This symposium discusses the difference between individual rights and collective rights with the special religious character of Israel's self-understanding as a collectivity in mind. Particular reference is made to the Arab minority in Israel.

002   Bick, Etta, ed. "Darchei Shalom." In her *Judaic Sources of Human Rights*, 45-87. Tel Aviv: Israel-Diaspora Institute, 1987.

> This part of Bick's anthology brings together several leading Jewish thinkers who analyze the principle of acting in such a way that peace increases in the world. The sessions focuses on biblical and rabbinic norms invoked for the sake of peace between religious groups. They review the discussion of whether Christianity should be considered an idolatrous religion. Some find the universal norm in Judaism to be the divine image in every human being. Some argue that since Jewish history interacts with world history, Jewish values embrace interaction with non-Jews.

003   Bick, Etta, ed. *Judaic Sources of Human Rights*. Tel Aviv: Israel-Diaspora Institute, 1987.

> This collection includes an introduction and prologue and a record of the dialogue between distinguished Israeli and American Jewish thinkers from various branches of organized Jewish life discussing the exceptional cases of Jewish law in which decisions are made on the basis of extraordinary principles. The book ends with

recommendations for how Jewish discussions can confront the ethical and moral dilemmas of modern times. See entries 069, 171, 193.

004   Bick, Etta, ed. "Pekuah Nefesh." In her *Judaic Sources of Human Rights*, 99-114. Tel Aviv: Israel-Diaspora Institute, 1987.

The principle of the overriding importance of saving a human life structures this discussion. This principle shows the interaction between Jewish law and the framework of that law. Some object saying that the idea of independent values is a late idea based on Kantian philosophy and not inherently Judaic.

005   Chapman, John W., and Pennock, J. Roland, eds. *Religion, Morality, and the Law*. Nomos 30. New York: New York University Press, 1988.

This anthology includes several philosophical studies of the meaning of morality, religion, and law which intersect an analysis of human rights. While as a whole the various essays provide a good perspective on the interaction of religion, morality, and theories of human rights, for Judaism in particular, see entry 078.

006   Cohn, Haim H. *Human Rights in Jewish Law*. New York: Ktav, 1984.

This study begins with a theoretical discussion of the relationship of rights and duties. The book divides into sections concerned with the rights of life, liberty and the pursuit of happiness, with rights of equality, the rights of justice. As an anthology this book serves as a useful reference work from which to begin a study of Judaism and human rights both historically considered and as applied in modern times. The various essays collected here reflect earlier writings by Cohn. See entries 067, 357, 433.

007   Elazar, Daniel J., ed. *Constitutionalism: The Israeli and American Experiences*. Lanham, MD: University Press of America, 1990.

This collection of essays, celebrating both Israel's fortieth year of existence as a modern state and the two hundredth anniversary of the United States Constitution explores how legal codes ensure the human rights of citizens. Several essays explore the Israeli debate about the desirability of a modern constitution. A consistent theme looks at human rights of conscience and religion, both in the United States and in Israel. The collection as a whole, then, reflects on the issues of religion, the Jewish conception of law, and the Jewish view of human rights. See entries 056, 106, 173, 204, 205, 286, 289, 614, 735, 751.

008   Esbeck, Carl H., ed. *Religious Beliefs, Human Rights, and the Moral Foundation of Western Democracy: 1986 Paine Lectures.* Columbia, MO: University of Missouri-Columbia Press, 1986.

This collection of three essays includes general reflections on the Judaic roots of the idea of human rights. The modern context, especially the American context, dominates each essay. Taken as a whole the collection shows how any theoretical discussion of human rights in contemporary life interweaves religious, biblical, and philosophical traditions. See entries 086, 551.

009   Gavison, Ruth, ed. *Civil Rights in Israel.* Jerusalem: The Association for Civil Rights in Israel, 1982. Hebrew.

This collection of essays in honor of Haim H. Cohn surveys the theory and practice of civil rights in Israel. The essays include reflection on how Jewish religion provides perspective on the idea of human rights. See entries 329, 347, 400, 617.

010   Hirsch, Emmanuel, ed. *Judaisme et Droits de l'Homme.* Idéologies et Droits de l'Homme B.01. Paris: Librairie des Libertés, 1984. French.

This anthology of essays collects writings on the general theory of human rights and Jewish thought and on specific issues in human rights. Some essays provide important analysis of Jewish texts and traditional Jewish theology. Other essays examine modern questions--such as the rights of women. Still others look at modern issues in the State of Israel. This collection offers an extremely valuable cross-section of Jewish thinking on the issue of human rights. See entries 041, 047, 048, 070, 080, 085, 095, 105, 110, 115, 189, 528, 706.

011   Kamenka, Eugene, and Erh-Soon Tay, Alice, eds. *Human Rights.* London: Edward Arnold, 1978.

This anthology includes a consideration of Jewish views on human rights and especially of Marx's views. It is particularly useful to see how the two different systems of understanding rights -- the Marxist and the classically Judaic interact. Even when not focused specifically on Jewish issues the articles in this anthology illuminate the diverse meanings thinkers attribute to the idea of universal rights. See entries 114, 233, 606.

012   Konvitz, Milton R., ed. *Judaism and Human Rights.* The B'nai B'rith Jewish Heritage Classics. New York: W. W. Norton, 1972.

Konvitz does not advance a coherent theory of human rights but gathers several articles concerned with issues of social justice such as equality, democracy, liberty, and peace. The various authors rarely raise the question of whether any of these indeed qualifies as a 'human right.' Two explicit articles speak of 'The right of privacy' and 'the right of dissent.' Taken as a whole, then, the book does offer a theory of human rights: Judaism represents a resource to which individuals can turn when seeking to establish the validity of their rights. See entries 058, 081, 102, 244, 503, 517.

013   Liberman, Serge, ed. *Anti-Semitism and Human Rights*. North Melbourne, Vic.: Australian Institute of Jewish Affairs, 1985.

Despite this title this collection of essays includes little direct reflection on the meaning of human rights. Several essays summarize the history of Jewish suffering under antisemitism, some look at the legal protection of human rights in certain countries, and all are helpful as background for a study of how antisemitism curtails Jewish rights. The majority of essays focus on the rights of the Jewish people, the national rights of a human collectivity, rather than the particular rights of individuals. See entries 142, 212, 368, 382, 602, 667, 691, 704, 705.

014   Liskofsky, Sidney, comp. *The United Nations and Human Rights--What are the Road Blocks: A Symposium*. New York: The American Jewish Committee, 1969.

This symposium includes the remarks by several diplomats, academics, and representatives of non-governmental organizations expressing both Jewish and non-Jewish concerns. Several contributions make explicit reference to the American Jewish situation and how American Jews apply the general ideal of human rights to issues such as antisemitism and Jews in the former Soviet Union and Israel.

015   Meron, Theodor, ed. *Human Rights in International Law: Legal and Policy Issues*. Oxford: Clarendon, 1984.

This anthology includes several essays of value in the study of Judaism and human rights. See entries 133, 265, 664.

016   Porter, Jack N., ed. *Genocide and Human Rights: A Global Anthology*. Washington, DC: University Press of America, 1982.

This anthology of essays includes considerable reference to the Jews in modern times, particular during the Nazi era. These works focus on the idea of genocide but also show how Jewish experience generates the concept of a crime against humanity. Such a concept implies that all human cultures have a right to exist.

017 Rakover, Nahum, ed. *Jewish Law and Current Legal Problems*. Library of Jewish Law. Jerusalem: Jewish Legal Heritage Society, 1984.

This anthology shows how Jewish law responds to modern problems and seeks to uphold the welfare and independence of the individual in the midst of society. While focused on specific questions of contemporary life, some of the articles make explicit reference to human rights.

018 Rouner, S. Leroy, ed. *Human Rights and World's Religions*. S. Leroy Rouner, series ed., Boston University Studies in Philosophy and Religion, 9. South Bend, IN: University of Notre Dame Press, 1988.

This useful collection of essays includes a helpful introduction by the editor that draws attention to the biblical and rabbinic perspective on human rights and suggests that religious views of human rights differ significantly from secular views. See entries 076. 125, 261, 530.

019 Shoham, Shlomo, ed. *Of Law and Man: Essays in Honor of Haim Cohn*. New York: Sabra, 1971.

This anthology includes several articles focused on the meaning of human rights. Several essays from this anthology appear in this present bibliography under varied rubrics, showing the comprehensiveness of the collection itself. See entries 065, 146.

020 Sidorsky, David, ed. *Essays on Human Rights: Contemporary Issues and Jewish Perspectives*. With Sidney Liskofsky and Jerome J. Shestack. Philadelphia: Jewish Publication Society, 1979.

This selection of essays examines theoretical questions about human rights, practical applications to specific situations such as those of Soviet Jews and Israeli Arabs, and views by Jewish writers from the biblical through the modern period. See entries 062, 071, 079, 160, 222, 223, 585, 609, 632, 636, 648.

021 Strauss, Leo, and Cropsey, Joseph, eds. *History of Political Philosophy*. Chicago: University of Chicago Press, 1987.

This useful textbook on political philosophy includes good background reading on the development of the idea of natural human rights. The introduction, bearing the stamp of Leo Strauss, and the article on Strauss make clear his own view of the impossibility of a religiously based theory of human rights and the connection of that view with his experience as a Jew.

022   Swersky, Ann, ed. *Human Rights in Israel: Articles in Memory of Judge Haman Shelah*. Tel Aviv: Edanim and Yediot Aharonot, 1988. Hebrew.

This collection of papers originally presented orally as a tribute to the memory of Haman Shelah combines theoretical studies on the idea of human rights with investigations of particular issues such as freedom of religion, free expression of dissent, tolerance for dissent, the position of the Arabs in Israel and of women in Jewish law. See entries 044, 122, 140, 215.

BIBLIOGRAPHIES AND ENCYCLOPEDIAS

023   Friedman, Julian R., and Sherman, Marc I., eds. *Human Rights: An International and Comparative Law Bibliography*. Bibliographies and Indexes in Law and Political Science 4. Westport, CT: Greenwood, 1985.

This bibliography is divided into two parts, one concerned with rights and the other with institutions, and draws extensively on articles in the *Israel Yearbook on Human Rights* and includes references of interest to the study of Judaism and human rights particularly in its sections on aliens, equality of treatment, human rights in general, self-determination, and genocide. The bibliography is particularly useful for tracing discussions of human rights violations either of Jews or by Israel, matters not immediately germane to the theoretical study of Judaism and human rights but of importance as a background to that study.

024   Lawson, Edward. *Encyclopedia of Human Rights*. New York: Taylor and Francis, 1989.

This reference work is notable more for what it does not contain than what it does. It includes several articles advancing the cause of Palestinian rights and criticizing the actions of Israel. It never mentions Judaism, persecution of Jews for their religion whether in the former Soviet Union or in Latin America. It fails to recognize the grounding of a modern human rights theory in Jewish tradition. The point made by including this entry is that no theory of human rights can be advanced without encompassing and acknowledging the way culturally specific values influence the identification of who does and does not fall under the category of those entitled to such rights.

025   Martin, Rex, and Nickel, James W. "A Bibliography on the Nature and
       Foundations of Human Rights. Legal Literature on International
       Human Rights." *Political Theory* 6, 3 (1978): 395-413.

       This short bibliography reveals the general neglect of bibliographers
       to recognize Jewish contributions to theories of human rights. While
       including several references to Christianity and human rights, the
       authors include no book or article explicitly concerned with the
       Jewish perspective on any of the issues covered. The closest subject
       matter chosen concerns the Enlightenment and Marxism.

026   Rakover, Nahum, ed. "Constitution, Human Rights." In his *A Bibliography
       of Jewish Law*, 147-148. Jerusalem: Harry Fischel Institute For
       Research in Jewish Law, 1975. Hebrew.

       This bibliography of Hebrew Language works on Jewish law
       includes several items of interest to the study of the theory of human
       rights in Judaism and a few investigations into specific questions.

027   Rakover, Nahum, ed. "Constitution, Human Rights." In his *A Bibliography
       of Jewish Law Part II*, 43-44. Jerusalem: Jewish Legal Heritage
       Society, 1990. Hebrew.

       Less useful than the preceding entry which it continues, this work
       indexes Ph.D. Dissertations, oral presentations, and informal
       lectures. Much of the material focuses on Israeli-Arab relationships.

028   Rakover, Nahum, ed. "Constitution, Human Rights." In his *The
       Multi-Language Bibliography of Jewish Law*, 365-369. Jerusalem:
       Jewish Legal Heritage Society, 1990.

       This bibliography of materials in languages other than Hebrew
       complements the preceding entries. While several entries do not
       focus clearly on rights but more broadly on themes such as
       individualism and social protest, this collection is highly useful for
       any study of Judaism and human rights.

029   Schonberg, David, and Weisbard, Phyllis Holman. *Human Rights Jewish
       Law: Bibliography of Sources and Scholarship in English*, 203-206.
       New York: Fred B. Rothman, 1989.

       More complete in its listing of English works than Rakover's
       volume, this bibliography also notes that 'human rights' is a modern
       phrase that finds no equivalent in Jewish legal terms but that its
       values pervade Jewish law as a whole. With this understanding it
       lists about forty entries.

030   Stanek, Edward. *Human Rights: A Selected Bibliography of Monographs, Essays, Serials and Basic Compilations of Documents and Bibliographies Pertinent to International Protection of Human Rights.* Public Administration Series: Bibliography, P21104. Monticello, IL: Vance Bibliographies, 1987.

The various entries focus on the practice of human rights less than on theoretical or theological concerns.   Some entries concern religious practice in the former Soviet Union, a concern in Jewish thinking about human rights; several provide useful background on Israeli treatment of Arabs and other ethnic minorities.

031   Vincent-Daviss, Diana, ed. *Selected Bibliography on Human Rights.* New York: New York University Press, 1980.

This bibliography includes some entries concerning Jews and Israel. The editor selects some references to Soviet Jews and several references to the Palestinian question but does not include the theoretical material found in more extensive works.

032   Wright, John T. "A Narrative Bibliography on Human Rights." In *Human Rights, Cultural and Ideological Perspectives*, eds. Adamantia Pollis and Peter Schwab, 145-149. New York: Praeger, 1979.

This bibliography reveals the neglect generally given to Jewish views on human rights.   While noting various journals, yearbooks, and annual studies on international human rights it fails to refer to the *Israel Yearbook on Human Rights*, one of the major annual studies that collects articles on a variety of human rights issues.

PERIODICALS AND JOURNALS

033   *Israel Law Review.* Israel: 1966.

This periodical has technical articles devoted to Jewish law, especially as practiced in modern Israel.   Despite its focus on the modern period it often includes reflections on theoretical issues of importance in the study of Judaism and human rights.

034   *Israel Yearbook on Human Rights.* Israel: 1971.

This annual publication is an invaluable source of information.   It records special conferences and seminars on specific issues concerning human rights.   Because of its Israeli venue it often includes articles of focusing on Jews and Judaism.

035   *The Jewish Law Annual*, ed. Bernard S. Jackson.   Leiden: Brill, 1978.

This scholarly publication dedicated to the study of Jewish law often raises important moral and ethical questions.   Essays by leading scholars deal with problems associated with the concept of human rights.   Each issue includes one section focused on an issue in Jewish law and a second part focusing on recent Israeli legal cases.

036   *Jewish Quarterly Review*, n.s. Philadelphia: Dropsie University, 1910.

Picking up after the demise of the first series in 1908, distributed by several different publishers during its course of publication, this periodical often includes articles illuminating how Jewish thinkers of the past responded to questions of human rights.   The high quality of the scholarship involved makes these articles of significance.

037   *Judaism*.   New York: American Jewish Congress, 1952.

While directed more at intelligent lay people than professionals, this journal has consistently included articles that probe intellectual problems associated with Jewish law, human rights, and the philosophy of Judaism.   Several seminal articles appeared first in this periodical and became anthologized thereafter.

038   *S'vara: A Journal of Philosophy and Judaism*.   New York: Columbia University School of Law and Shalom Hartman Institute. 1991.

More popular than *The Jewish Law Annual* in both format and content, this very recent publication often includes articles devoted to current issues.   These issues often have particular relevance for a study of human rights.

039   *Tel Aviv University Law Review (Iyyunei Mishpat)*.   Israel: 1971.   Hebrew.

This Hebrew language periodical from Tel Aviv University focuses on issues of interest to lawyers in Israel.   Nevertheless, frequent essays address more general questions such as those concerning human rights.

040   *Tradition*.   New York: 1958.

An official journal of the Union of American Orthodox Congregations, this periodical includes reflection on current issues from the perspective of traditional Judaism.   It often illuminates the legal background of Jewish moral and ethical thinking, including reflection on the idea of human rights.

2

Human Rights in the Bible and Talmud

041   Agi, Marc. "Judaisme et Droits de l'Homme." In *Judaisme et Droits de l'Homme*, ed. Emmanuel Hirsch, 3-21. Idéologies et Droits de l'Homme B.01. Paris: Librairie des Libertés, 1984. French.

     The development of the idea of human rights from the biblical ten commandments to modern formulations, Agi concludes, consists in a growing concretization of certain vague notions. He points to the Noahide laws in Judaism, the requirement to love the neighbor as the self, certain prophetic calls for justice, and rabbinic affirmations of the importance of human life to show that Judaism cultivates the notion from which the modern view of human rights develops.

042   Ahroni, Reuben. "The Levirate and Human Rights." *Jewish Law and Current Legal Problems*, ed. Nahum Rakover, 67-76. Library of Jewish Law. Jerusalem: Jewish Legal Heritage Society, 1984.

     Ahroni argues that the present exercise of the levirate laws leaves a woman without her right to remarry. The employment of this biblical practice in a modern context actually infringes on a woman's human rights both to have a family and to make a free choice. The Bible, itself, he thinks, advances the law to ensure the preservation of those rights. He, therefore, suggests changes in the modern use of that law.

043   Bamberger, Bernard. "Individual Rights and the Demands of the State: The Position of Classical Judaism." *Central Conference of American Rabbis Yearbook* 54 (1955): 197-212.

     Modern thinkers have rejected the social contract theory on which the idea of human rights was founded. The Bible, however, bases its views of human rights on religious grounds: the dignity of the human being and freedom of the individual. Thus the Bible pits the law of the state against the law of God, not against the rights of the individual. Medieval Jewish communities did not define individual rights clearly but the practical results of Torah law accord closely with the goals of 'the Rights of Man.'

044   Bar Navi, Eli. "Civil Rights--a Historical Perspective." In *Human Rights in Israel: Articles in Memory of Judge Haman Shelah*, ed. Ann Swersky, 11-21. Tel Aviv: Edanim and Yediot Aharonot, 1988. Hebrew.

This essay is remarkable for its omissions no less than its valuable historical sketch. Bar-Navi contends that the idea of natural human rights is a modern notion, drawing on a combination of Greek philosophical concepts and Christian medieval theology. He does not include the biblical material in his review of pre-modern sources of the idea of human rights. He offers a survey of modern criticisms of liberalism and its espousal of rights, but concludes that democracy provides the best environment for the protection of rights. He brings in specifically Jewish experience only in the recent period from World War II through developments in the modern State of Israel.

045   Bar-Zev, Asher. "Euthanasia: A Classical Ethical Problem in a Modern Context." *Reconstructionist* 44, 9-10 (1979): 7-16, 7-10.

Bar-Zev notes that Jewish tradition emphasizes the primacy of life by surveying biblical and rabbinic views. He contrasts this with other secular and religious points of view. He details the variations found in Jewish response.

046   Bardfelt, Philip A. "Jewish Medical Ethics." *Reconstructionist* 42, 6 (1976): 7-11.

While entitled medical ethics this essay focuses on the issue of euthanasia, the precedents found in Jewish history such as the suicide of King Saul, and the differences between actively enabling death and passively removing obstacles to it.

047   Barnet, Kriegel Blandine. "Judaisme et Droit de l'Homme." In *Judaisme et Droits de l'Homme*, ed. Emmanuel Hirsch, 127-131. Idéologies et Droits de l'Homme. Paris: Librairie des Libertés, 1984. French.

While Rome is the source of Western law, it is not the source of Western respect for human dignity. The idea of human rights requires three basic elements: the valuation of each person, a statutory law articulating that value, and a political community enforcing that law. Biblical teachings are an essential component in the modern idea of human rights. The influence of Hebrew thought on such modern thinkers as Hobbes and Spinoza helped establish those elements in Western life.

048   Baruk, Henri. "Droits et Devoirs Dan La Tradition Hebraique." In *Judaisme et Droits de l'Homme*, ed. Emmanuel Hirsch, 23-38. Idéologies et Droits de l'Homme. Paris: Librairie des Libertés, 1984. French.

Baruk notes the tension between Judaism's emphasis on duties and its respect for human rights in both biblical and rabbinic texts. He concludes that rights without duties are meaningless since rights serve to create the framework within which duties may be performed. Duties without rights are equally empty since the purpose of duties is to guarantee the protection of the rights of others.

049   Belkin, Samuel. "The Community." In his *In His Image: The Jewish Philosophy of Man as Expressed in Rabbinic Tradition*, 117-133. Westport, CT: Greenwood, 1979.

According to Belkin, both biblical and rabbinic law balance the rights of the community against the individual's right to privacy. He discusses "rights of neighbors" which he considers an application of the rule that people are responsible to others. He draws an interesting connection between every individual's right to privacy and the right to peace.

050   Belkin, Samuel. "The Equality of Man." In his *In His Image: The Jewish Philosophy of Man as Expressed in Rabbinic Tradition*, 60-78. Westport, CT: Greenwood, 1979.

Belkin considers how biblical and rabbinic law established the principle of equality as a basic part of social organization.

051   Belkin, Samuel. *In His Image: The Jewish Philosophy of Man as Expressed in Rabbinic Tradition*, Westport, CT: Greenwood, 1979.

Several important sections of this book deal explicitly with human rights and other parts have clear implications for a theory of rights. Gershon Weiler, then, is a bit misleading when citing (see entry 151, p. 171) Belkin's lack of reference to rights.

052   Belkin, Samuel. "Man and His Trustworthiness." In his *In His Image: The Jewish Philosophy of Man as Expressed in Rabbinic Tradition*, 79-96. Westport, CT: Greenwood, 1979.

In the course of investigating biblical and rabbinic law, Belkin establishes various legal rights as fundamental to all human social order.

053   Belkin, Samuel. "The Sacredness of Human Life." In his *In His Image: The Jewish Philosophy of Man as Expressed in Rabbinic Tradition*, 97-116. Westport, CT: Greenwood, 1979.

Belkin surveys the sacredness of human life in both biblical and rabbinic sources and discovers in this principle several duties that result in certain human rights. Among these he emphasizes a person's right to life, dignity, personal liberty, and several rights associated with the employer and employee relationship. Important parts of this chapter include a consideration of "man's right to dignity" and "the right of personal liberty."

054   Berman, Saul J. "The Status of Women in Halakhic Judaism." *Tradition* 1 (1973): 5-18.

Berman reviews biblical and postbiblical Jewish texts and points to three issues raised by the status of women in Judaism. Among them he discusses the legal disadvantages women face. Thus women often find their human rights denied. He argues for change in Jewish law to resolve this problem. This essay is reproduced in *The Jewish Woman: New Perspectives*, ed. Elizabeth Koltun. New York: Schocken, 1976, pp. 114-128.

055   Bick, Etta, ed. "Darchei Shalom." In her *Judaic Sources of Human Rights*, 45-87. Tel Aviv: Israel-Diaspora Institute, 1987.

See the annotation at entry 002.

056   Blaustein, Albert. "Contemporary Trends in Constitution - Writing." In *Constitutionalism: The Israeli and American Experiences*, ed. Daniel J. Elazar, 171-177. Lanham, MD: University Press of America, 1990.

Blaustein emphasizes the Jewish tradition of constitution-writing from the biblical period through the present day. He describes modern constitutions from the American and French examples in the eighteenth century through more modern ones, and what are called the three generations of human rights: political, economic and social, and developmental. He concludes by noting the presence of a "rich Talmudic as well as a rich democratic tradition" on which to draw.

057   Bleich, J. David. "Judaism and Natural Law." *Jewish Law Annual* 7 (1988): 5-42.

Bleich explains the rabbinic principles of the Noahide laws and that of the Law of the secular authority is considered as binding as Torah Law as part of an argument that law manifests rationality. Thus he suggests reason implies certain universal principles and a divine design for humanity. In this way reason itself demands that human beings seek for the divine.

058   Bokser, Ben Zion. "Democratic Aspirations in Talmudic Judaism." In *Judaism and Human Rights*, ed. Milton R. Konvitz, 145-155. New York: W. W. Norton, 1972.

The author reviews the classic literature of rabbinic Judaism to find its inherently democratic nature. He claims that reciprocal responsibilities are the basis of mutual obligations among human beings. The various spheres covered by human rights are, thus, spheres of interrelationships not of absolute liberties. He illustrates this claim by examples of the mutualities linking workers to their employers, joining the various strata of social administration, uniting members of a family and creating bonds between citizens and their nation.

059   Borowitz, Eugene B. *Renewing the Covenant: Theology for the Postmodern Jew*. Philadelphia: Jewish Publication Society, 1991.

Borowitz explores the balance between autonomy and acceptance of obligations as part of a Jew's experience under the covenant with God. He considers the interaction of particularism and universalism and touches on several important questions of human rights. He raises the challenge of feminism in many parts of this book. He emphasizes a commitment to woman's equality while allowing women to articulate their sense of their own rights. He summarizes Michael Wyschogrod's view of the rights of conscience deriving from a divinely given innate sense of justice but notes that it has won few Orthodox Jewish followers. He provides three examples of where the commitment of American Jews to the rights of individuals to self-determination, freedom of movement, and to be different led them to reject the demands of Israeli leaders. Most significantly he places Jewish covenantal duties within the framework of the universal human duties expressed symbolically in tradition by the idea of the Noahide covenant. In this way Jewish rights are an extension of the universal rights of humanity. Various essays shed light on the classical sources of Jewish thought such as the Bible and Talmud.

060   Borowitz, Eugene B. "Social Justice, the Liberal Jewish Case." In his *Exploring Jewish Ethics: Papers on Covenant Responsibility*, 295-307. Detroit, MI: Wayne State University Press, 1990.

Borowitz notes that while Jews easily affirm the abstract ideals of biblical ethics, translating them into concrete moral decision is more difficult. Nevertheless, Jews refuse to abandon the quest for universal values. Without a single standard of human goodness, like the idea of human rights, they cannot criticize governments such as that of the Nazis. A modern Jewish social agenda must balance abstraction and concrete application, universalism and particularism.

061   Borowitz, Eugene B. "The Torah, Written and Oral, and Human Rights: Foundations and Deficiencies." In *The Ethics of World Religions and Human Rights*, eds. Hans Küng and Jürgen Moltmann, 25-33. London: SCM, 1990.

Borowitz begins by noting that the idea that human beings have any rights other than those specifically granted by the divine being is nearly blasphemy. He continues by showing both the religious grounds for believing that human beings possess certain rights and the problems of making that assertion on the basis of a particularistic tradition. He also notes that recent Jewish history reinforces the ultimate value of universal human rights. He draws on biblical and Talmudic sources as well as on modern Jewish experience.

062   Brichto, Herbert Chanan. "The Bible on Human Rights." In *Essays in Human Rights: Contemporary Issues and Jewish Perspectives*, eds. David Sidorsky, *et al.*, 215-233. Philadelphia: Jewish Publication Society, 1979.

Brichto argues against the linguistic argument for the absence of human rights in the Bible, claiming that the Bible sets out a charter of almost absolute rights. Nevertheless, he admits, the biblical ideal is tempered by an appreciation of the existential facts that prevent its realization. He concludes that the Bible evinces concern for human rights by structuring humanistic values in society. He identifies human rights with the combination of these values, rather than with an abstract concept presumed to be either evident or non-existent.

063   Carmi, Amnon. "To Live Like A King: Die Like A King." In his *Law and Medicine*, 28-63. Haifa: Tamar, 1987.

This excellent study of euthanasia in Jewish thought contains a lengthy and useful bibliography. Carmi shows how the record of Saul's death inspired several different interpretations ranging from suicide to punishment. Looking at the issue from the more general perspective of human rights as such, he notes that humanity, according to Jewish thought, is characterized by its moral responsibility. He concludes that both death and life should represent and express human dignity.

064   Carmilly-Weinberger, Moshe. *Book and Sword: Freedom of Expression and Thought Among the Jewish People*. New York: Shulsinger Brothers, 1966. Hebrew.

The book traces freedom of expression in the media as expressed in Jewish law from the Rabbis through medieval and modern thought. It pays close attention to the response given to heretics such as the Sabbatians, Reform Jews, and modern idéologies. It concludes by surveying specific Israeli newspapers and periodicals and their interaction with free speech.

065   Cassin, René. "From the Ten Commandments to the Rights of Man." In *Of Law and Man: Essays in Honor of Haim Cohn*, ed. Shlomo Shoham, 13-25. New York: Sabra, 1971.

Cassin acknowledges that no formal relation between the modern concept of human rights and the Ten Commandments exists. He suggests, however, that the affirmation of human dignity began with the Ten Commandments and only later developed into a secular form. After World War II, he contends, the need for a formal declaration of human rights grew. He finds in the impetus for such a declaration the expression of the Jewish passion for justice.

066   Cohen, Alfred S. "Privacy: A Jewish Perspective." *Journal of Halakha and Contemporary Society* 1 (1980): 53-102.

Cohen notes the negative and positive approaches in which privacy is either protected from intrusion or proactively protected. The latter approach characterizes the examples Cohen gives of rabbinic teaching prohibiting intrusion on an individual or on the home. Cohen also notes the different standard used when public figures are involved. This article is reprinted in *Halacha and Contemporary Society* , ed. Alfred S. Cohen, New York: Ktav, 1984, 193-242.

067   Cohn, Haim H. "Discriminations of Women." In his Human Rights in Jewish Law, 167-177. New York: Ktav, 1984.

Cohn argues that Jewish law infringes on women's rights. Rabbinic restrictions prevent a woman from full participation in legal procedures, discriminate against a wife in domestic conflicts, and produce harmful and misleading stereotypes. Cohn argues his case on the basis of a broad conception of human rights in Jewish thought.

068   Cohn, Haim H. *Human Rights in the Bible and Talmud*. Jerusalem: Ministry of Security, 1988. Hebrew.

Cohn traces the theory of human rights in Judaism from its biblical and rabbinic sources.   He shows how these sources advocate universal rights for all human beings.   His essays include a useful review of Jewish sources and a liberal perspective on human rights.

069   Cohn, Haim H. "Introduction." In *Judaic Sources of Human Rights*, ed. Etta Bick, 1-15. Tel Aviv: Israel-Diaspora Institute, 1987.

Cohn discusses the balance between leniency and rigor among Jewish legalists. He notes that talmudic scholars legitimated deviations from the letter of the law, initiated concessions to the needs of the times, and created general principles to ensure human rights.   While he feels the discussion collected in the book shows the pluralism of Torah, he thinks it failed to unite the participants whom, he thought, were not yet really capable of listening to one another in open dialogue.

070   Cohn, Haim H. "La Liberté de Pensée et de Parole en Droit Juif." In *Judaisme et Droits de l'Homme*, ed. Emmanuel Hirsch, 54-83. Idéologies et Droits de l'Homme, B.01. Paris: Librairie des Libertés, 1984. French.

Cohn (because of the vagaries of transliteration from Hebrew, the name is spelled 'Cohen' in this volume; I use the more normal spelling for this person's name) notes that the Bible and Talmud allow restrictions on free speech for moral and religious purposes. Despite these restrictions, he points to the Hebrew prophets, rabbinic tolerance for such heretics as Elisha ben Abuya and Eliezer ben Hyrcanus to demonstrate a tradition of free speech. He surveys the darker picture of the excommunication of Spinoza, the Maimonidean Controversy, and other challenges to the ideal of free speech.

071   Daube, David. "The Rabbis and Philo on Human Rights." In *Human Rights in Essays on Human Rights: Contemporary Issues and Jewish Perspectives*, ed. David Sidorsky, *et al.*, 234-246. Philadelphia: Jewish Publication Society, 1979.

While lacking an exact term for human rights, both rabbinic literature and Philo seek to protect human dignity, justice, and the ways of peace. He notes that suicide is not reproved in the scriptural tradition.

072   Dorff, Elliot N. "Defensive War." *S'vara: A Journal of Philosophy and Judaism* 1, 2 (1991): 25-29.

Dorff, drawing on classic Jewish sources, raises the question of whether the individual's right to self-defense translates into a community's right to defend itself through a defensive war. He notes all the restrictions that Jewish law places on the waging of such a war. He argues for the justification of preemptive strikes but recognizes situations in which what begins as a justified strike becomes untenable after a lengthy occupation.

073 Falk, Zeev W. "Human Rights." In his *Law and Religion: The Jewish Experience*, 75-89. Jerusalem: Mesharim, 1981. Hebrew.

Falk traces the development of human sensitivity to others from kinship solidarity to an affirmation of general human rights. He sees theology as the basic foundation for the concept of human rights. He claims that the presumption of such rights precedes the description of duties of one person to another. He admits that the Jewish experience with Gentiles often led to a lack of recognition of universal rights, but he thinks the Jewish approach from Philo through the modern period was basically positive. He notes the problem the state of Israel finds in granting non-conforming Jews the right of freedom from religion.

074 Finkelstein, Louis. "The Hebrew Doctrine of Equality." *Menorah Journal* 24 (1936): 16-29.

Finkelstein focuses on the Hebrew prophets as self-conscious protests against discrimination. He traces the difference between rural and urban sensitivities to violations of human rights.

075 Finkelstein, Louis. "Human Equality in the Jewish Tradition." *Conservative Judaism* 10, 1 (1955): 1-27.

Finkelstein reviews prophetic and rabbinic statements concerning equality of human rights under the Noahide laws, the meaning of the selection of the Jewish people, the importance of civil rights, and general rights of justice. He takes the principle of the human being as a servant of God to be the basis for human rights and concludes that these rights are merely ethical norms that cannot be enforced by society.

076 Fishbane, Michael. "The Image of the Human and the Rights of the Individual in Jewish Tradition." In *Human Rights and World's Religions*, ed. Leroy S. Rouner, 17-32. Leroy S. Rouner, series ed., Boston University Studies in Philosophy and Religion, 9. South Bend, IN: University of Notre Dame Press, 1988.

Fishbane stresses the absolute worth of every human being as a distinctive view of Israelite society that is continued and strengthened in later Jewish thought. He stresses that the so-called Noahide laws provide a common basis for human rights that transcends specifically Jewish limits. He does note, however, that historical conditions explain why one or another Jewish community suspends or limits rights for several reasons--gender related issues curtail the rights of women, the demand of higher duties curtail less exalted rights. He concludes that while some aspects of the Jewish system of rights may be historically conditioned, the theory's basic contribution is as a resource pointing to the basis of any theory of human rights: the shared sense of human personhood that transcends individual self-interest.

077   Fox, Marvin. "Maimonides and Aquinas on Natural Law." *Dine Israel* 3 (1973)

Fox traces the Jewish resistance to a theory of natural law, citing the view of Leo Strauss that the Bible contains no theory of natural rights. He focuses attention on Maimonides' treatment of the Noahide laws and does not find in them a theory of universal human rights. He contrasts this approach with that of Christianity which, by rejecting the laws of the Hebrew Scripture needed a new basis for those principles upon which a social order depends. This essay also appears in his *Interpreting Maimonides: Studies in Methodology, Metaphysics and Moral Philosophy*. Chicago: University Press of Chicago, 1990, pp. 124-151.

078   Garet, Ronald R. "Natural Law and Creation Stories." In *Religion, Morality, and the Law*, eds. J. Roland Pennock and John W. Chapman, 218-262. Nomos 30. New York: New York University Press, 1988.

Garet notes that the idea of natural law depends upon an idea of nature and looks at natural rights and natural commands. By natural rights he means a theory of nature concerning the good life for humanity and the just regime in society most hospitable to that life. He suggests rabbinic and biblical discussions of natural law and contrasts them with Christian and Greek ideas. He also studies the idea of the image of God and its application to a view of rights. He criticizes Leo Strauss for claiming that the Hebrew Bible has no view of nature. While lacking a philosophy of nature it does provide the basis for the idea of natural law.

079   Goitein, S. D. "Human Rights in Jewish Thought and Life in the Middle Ages." In *Essays on Human Rights: Contemporary Issues and Jewish Perspectives*, eds. David Sidorsky, *et al.*, 247-264. Philadelphia: Jewish Publication Society, 1979.

Goitein emphasizes that philosophers recognized that only an orderly society provided the environment for the ideal life to which they aspired. Under the influence of Muslim thought a greater concern for human rights theory developed as exemplified in changing laws about slavery, communal rights, the rights of women, and domestic relationships in general, and the rights of the needy. Commercial intercourse made Jews sensitive to human relations. The basis of human rights was not God but human brotherhood.

080   Goldmann, Alain. "Les Sources Juives des Droits de l'Homme." In *Judaisme et Droits de l'Homme*, ed. Emmanuel Hirsch, 45-51. Idéologies et Droits de l'Homme   B.01. Paris: Librairie des Libertés, 1984. French.

Goldmann suggests that while the technical term 'human rights' does not occur in biblical and rabbinic literature, the idea is clearly present. He shows how passages from that literature address the unity of humanity, the love of the stranger, the right to safety from fear, economic rights, and respect for the human person.

081   Gordis, Robert. "The Right of Dissent and Intellectual Liberty." In *Judaism and Human Rights*, ed. Milton R. Konvitz, 190-211. New York: W. W. Norton, 1972.

Gordis suggests that postbiblical Judaism tempers its pressure for conformity with an advocacy of the right to dissent. He points to the biblical origins of this right in the prophets and its development in teachings of the oral law as shown by preservation of both the schools of Shammai and Hillel. He remarks that Judaism uses the ban or excommunication only to preserve religious and ethical standards or to preserve the Jewish system or to punish official abuse of authority. Although Jews did not always abide by this ideal Gordis claims that it still remains operative.

082   Greenberg, Moshe. "Rabbinic Reflections on Defying Illegal Orders: Amasa, Abner, and Joab." In *Contemporary Jewish Ethics*, ed. Menahem M. Kellner, 211-220.   David M. L. Olivestone, series ed., Sanhedrin Jewish Studies. New York: Sanhedrin, 1978.

Greenberg reviews the rabbinic interpretation of various biblical examples of dissent from authority and notes the limitations placed on the rights of the state by Jewish law even during warfare. The article includes useful references to both biblical texts and rabbinic interpretations of them. These references form the basis for a theory of both the right to dissent and the right to live in peace.

083   Guttmann, Alexander. "The Role of Equity in the History of the Halakhah." In *Julius Mark Jubilee Volume*, eds. Ronald Sobel and Sidney Wallach, 71-92. New York: Ktav, 1975.

This study looks at the sensitivity with which rabbinic law sought to ensure equity in various cases where a strict enforcement of law might undermine the practice of equality.   Guttmann considers several cases involving a putative inequality extended to women: the case of the woman suspected of adultery, of entering marriage without her virginity, the exclusion of women from certain observances, and questions of marriage and divorce.   He notes however that various legal authorities decide cases in conformity with equity without, however, admitting that the concern for equality actually motivated their decisions.   This article is reproduced in his *Studies in Rabbinic Judaism*, New York: Ktav, 1976, 261-282.

084   Harrelson, Walter. *The Ten Commandments and Human Rights*. Overtures to Biblical Theology. Philadelphia: Fortress, 1980.

Despite its title and despite the discussion of several issues pertinent to the study of human rights, this book does not focus on human rights as such.   Instead it explores the modern meaning of the obligations and prohibitions found in the Ten Commandments primarily from a Christian perspective. The appendix includes the Universal Declaration of Human Rights.

085   Hassoun, Jacques. "Le Role du Kahal dans L'Education aux Droits de l'Homme." In *Judaisme et Droits de l'Homme*, ed. Emmanuel Hirsch, 119-125. Idéologies et Droits de l'Homme B.01. Paris: Librairie des Libertés, 1984. French.

Hassoun claims that the Jews as a community play a significant role in the history of the modern development of human rights.   Several revolutionary Jewish groups in the modern age, he claims, advanced the idea of rights. Even in the pre-modern period the Jewish idea of community in the Bible, the rabbis, and the Council of the Four Lands shows a receptivity to the rights of humanity that is the mark of an aptitude for civilization and social organization.

086   Henry, Carl F. H. "The Judeo-Christian Heritage and Human Rights." In *Religious Beliefs, Human Rights, and the Moral Foundation of Western Democracy: 1986 Paine Lectures*, ed. Carl H. Esbeck, 27-40. Columbia, MO: University of Missouri-Columbia Press, 1986.

Henry surveys ancient civilizations and their views of rights and judges the biblical tradition the most exemplary.   He agrees that biblical law generally emphasizes duties rather than rights, but points out notable exceptions. Human dignity, he claims, is a right cherished in the biblical and Jewish traditions. The primary thrust of his essay is to show that modern thinking about human rights draws on the biblical religious traditions found in the North American context.

087 Heschel, Abraham Joshua. "A Declaration of Conscience." In his *The Insecurity of Freedom: Essays on Human Existence*, 274-284. New York: Schocken, 1972.

Heschel reviews the long history of Jews in Russia, changes that he recently witnessed in the Soviet Union, and the biblical precedent for being concerned with others. He uses this precedent to demonstrate a continuing Jewish commitment to the right of individuals to self-determination. He calls upon all people to advocate the rights of Soviet Jews since "To fight for human rights is to save our own souls," p. 283. He claims a Jewish legacy for the demand that all people receive equal treatment.

088 Heschel, Abraham Joshua. *The Insecurity of Freedom: Essays on Human Existence*. New York: Schocken, 1972.

These several essays culled from different sources and given on different occasions provide a Jewish perspective on various modern social and moral problems. Throughout the book Heschel argues that rights are more than "legalized interests." Instead they are the groundwork for human obligations. Several essays provide biblical and rabbinic sources reflecting on the nature of being human and the rights and obligations flowing from that nature. The collection as a whole testifies to Heschel's commitment to both traditional values and the transformation of present-day society. He refuses to limit Jewish principles to a pre-determined program from the past or to limit resources for solving contemporary problems to those of secular modernity.

089 Heschel, Abraham Joshua. "Jews in the Soviet Union." In his *The Insecurity of Freedom: Essays on Human Existence*, 262-273. New York: Schocken, 1972.

Heschel compares the battle for Soviet Jews to the struggle waged by American blacks to gain their civil liberties. Citing both biblical and rabbinic precedent he argues that all humanity shares in the responsibility for ameliorating the problems of Soviet Jews.

090   Heschel, Abraham Joshua. "The Patient as Person." In his *The Insecurity of Freedom: Essays on Human Existence*, 24-38. New York: Schocken, 1972.

Basing himself on biblical and rabbinic precepts, Heschel argues that a person's right to health includes the right to humane treatment as a unique individual and not merely as a collection of symptoms. His basic principle of a religious humanism that protects rights so as to ensure an ability to serve the divine manifests itself in both the area of treating the ill and preserving life.

091   Heschel, Abraham Joshua. "Religion and Race." In his *The Insecurity of Freedom: Essays on Human Existence*, 85-100. New York: Schocken, 1972.

Heschel argues that religion stands against all racism. He uses biblical and rabbinic examples to show the incompatibility of religion with refusing rights to any human community. While the right to equality is important, Heschel emphasizes the even greater issue: the scandal of inequality. Thus he shows how a Jewish humanism inspires actions that ensure the protection of each person's right to equal treatment and prevent the denial of rights based on a person's racial identity.

092   Heschel, Abraham Joshua. "Religion in a Free Society." In his *The Insecurity of Freedom: Essays on Human Existence*, 3-23. New York: Schocken, 1972.

Heschel argues that rights must be understood in terms of human needs. He uses rabbinic sources to show that religion teaches how to transform needs into an opportunity to perceive human obligations to others.

093   Heschel, Abraham Joshua. "Sacred Image of Man." In his *The Insecurity of Freedom: Essays on Human Existence*, 150-167. New York: Schocken, 1972.

Weaving together rabbinic and biblical stories and motifs Heschel argues for the dignity of every human being and the equality of each person based on that dignity. Although focused on the right to equal treatment, this essay offers a complete theory of rights generally. Rights derive from each person's potential to fulfill a vital role in the divine plan. Human beings are granted rights because without them individuals could not perform the task that God demands of them.

094   Heschel, Abraham Joshua. "The White Man on Trial." In his *The Insecurity of Freedom: Essays on Human Existence*, 101-111. New York: Schocken, 1972.

Heschel, employing the rhetoric of biblical and rabbinic writings, declares the problem of blacks in America as a sickness, symptomatic of the problems in America generally. Black Americans must be granted equal rights not only because racism is an evil but also because racism undermines true religion. A society that allows race to deprive citizens of the right to equal treatment demonstrates its insensitivities to the value of every individual, a value that Jewish sources unmistakably affirms.

095   Israel, Rachel. "Judaisme et Dissidence." In *Judaisme et Droits de l'Homme*, ed. Emmanuel Hirsch, 189-198. Paris: Librairie des Libertés, 1984. French.

Rachel Israel shows that the idea of rights and obligations develops as part of the theory of asocial contract. The reality, however, suggests that nations are not formed on such a basis and that social discontent arises in most nations. She reviews how Jewish literature records such dissent in the revolt of Korah against Moses and in Samuel's dictum: the Law of the Kingdom is Jewish law. She describes Jewish minority status in the Roman empire, in medieval times, and today in the USSR, showing how persecution highlights the gap between law and reality and thus leads eventually to an affirmation of human rights. She does not explicitly claim that this Jewish history created a theory of human rights, but does find the roots of a theory granting all people rights to equal treatment and to the power of dissent in various Jewish texts from the Bible through classical rabbinic literature. Thus, implicitly, she suggests that the Jewish theory of human rights is one that arises in response to the pressures and challenges of history and seeks to make social life possible even in pluralistic communities.

096   Kaplan, Abraham. "Human Relations and Human Rights in Judaism." In *The Philosophy of Human Rights: International Perspectives*, ed. Alan S. Rosenbaum, 53-85. Contributions in Philosophy 15. Westport, CT: Greenwood, 1980.

The author focuses on doctrine and not on codes and argues that human rights flow from the nature of being human as established by the divinity. He cites rabbinic views of human dignity, laws preserving that dignity, philosophical doctrines of human nature, and Hasidic exaltations of the human being. He thinks of Judaism as morally individualistic and rejects the pejorative implication of 'tribalism' as a description of Jewish morality while admitting the importance of the community in Jewish thinking. He stresses Jewish universalism and rationalism.

097   Kaplan, Mordecai M. *Judaism Without Supernaturalism: The Only Alternative to Orthodoxy and Secularism*. New York: Reconstructionist, 1967.

Kaplan claims that religions must advocate the inalienable right that each person enjoys to become fully self-actualized. He argues that the Bible anticipated the American Bill of Rights when prophets, lawgivers, and sages contended that individuals and groups have the absolute right of making the most of themselves.

098   Kaplan, Mordecai M. *The Meaning of God in Jewish Religion*. New York: Reconstructionist, 1962.

Kaplan argues for the sacredness of human rights rather than for a theory of natural rights. He claims that we have rights because without them we cannot fulfill our obligations in the life of human society. Rights emanate from the attributes of personality and thus from God as the force by which people become most fully persons. The first essential right is the conception of property, and Kaplan claims that it is symbolized by the Jewish holiday of Sukkot -- a protest against a competitive and profit-seeking impulse that undermines human self-achievement. He then contends that the holiday of Passover celebrates a related right, that of being oneself.

099   Katz, Nathan. "Jewish Perspectives on Equality." *Ethnic Studies Report* IV, 1 (January 1986): 64-70.

Reviewing biblical, rabbinic, and mystical Jewish materials, Katz surveys Jewish thinking on the idea of equality and its relationship to the idea that one reaches God through interaction with other human beings. He emphasizes the "right to life" as taking precedence over other rights. He argues for the equal right to chosenness--all peoples can claim their special chosenness without displacing the chosenness of others.

100   Kimmelman, Reuven. "Nonviolence in the Talmud." *Judaism* 17 (1968): 316-334.

Kimmelman insists that peace and justice often demand taking violent action and that Judaism, therefore, is not pacifist when defending human rights. He supports this argument by citing biblical and rabbinic Jewish sources. His basic contention, then, suggests that Judaism has a theory of justice, not a theory of human rights.

Human rights, however, represent one subcategory of justice for which Jewish thought demands often activist and violent protection.

101   Kimmelman, Reuven. "The Rabbinic Ethics of Protest." *Judaism* 19 (1970): 38-58.

Kimmelman surveys the rabbinic teachings about political dissent in the name of transcendent values of human rights. He concludes that the rabbis circumscribed political protest as a means of attaining human rights. In this case abrogation of one putative right -- that to dissent -- becomes a means for securing all other rights, above all the right to develop as a human being. The theory of human rights espoused, then, is that of pursuing a life of justice and attachment to the transcendent. In such a theory the mundane political right to dissent may be sacrificed for a greater good.

102   Konvitz, Milton R. "Man's Dignity in God's World." In his *Judaism and Human Rights*, 27-32. New York: W. W. Norton, 1972.

The author emphasizes how the biblical creation stories and their view of humanity as partner with the divine, both indispensable but also not coerced into service, establish a theory of human rights. The polarity of humanity as both a creator and creature leads Judaism to emphasize that people possess dignity but should act with humility. Konvitz claims that this duality is the foundation for an individual's right to live as an individual but also the right of others that their lives be respected as well.

103   Konvitz, Milton R. "Torah and Constitution : An American Bicentennial Lecture." *Proceedings of the Rabbinical Assembly* 38 (1976): 54-67.

This essay suggests the convergence of American and Jewish values. It presents a general theory of human rights as a political and legal principle and a specific theory about law. The principle of rule by law rather than by power does not clearly appear based on a theory of universal human rights.   Konvitz claims that the Jewish Bible presents a model of how lawfulness protects individual human freedoms. It suggests that appeal to law secures each person's rights. Everyone, then, has a basic right to access to the law according to both biblical and American precedent and lawfulness itself represents the basic ideal on which the rights of the individual depend. This article is reprinted in his *Judaism and the American Idea*, New York: Schocken, 1980, 53-68.

104   Kushner, Harold S. "A Jewish View of Verbal and Visual Obscenity." *Proceedings of the Rabbinical Assembly* 40 (1978): 102-107.

Kushner notes how Jewish religious sensitivities caused changes in basic texts such as the Bible and the Talmud. These self-conscious alterations of tradition show the importance Jewish tradition places on preventing embarrassment. In the conflict between Judaism and Paganism such sensitivity is necessary, he avers, and suggests that in today's world censorship of obscenity is a necessary Jewish value that enhances rather than impairs human rights.

105   Landau, Lazare. "Judaisme et Droits de l'Homme." In *Judaisme et Droits de l'Homme*, ed. Emmanuel Hirsch, 59-63. Idéologies et Droits de l'Homme B.01. Paris: Librairie des Libertés, 1984. French.

Landau traces the development of the modern idea of human rights to its roots in biblical universalism and the talmudic stress on human dignity.

106   Landau, Moshe. "The Limits of Constitutions and Judicial Review." In *Constitutionalism: The Israeli and American Experiences*, ed. Daniel J. Elazar, 197-205. Lanham, MD: University Press of America, 1990.

Landau argues that the Jewish system combines the idea of justice, respect for law, and a system of duties that protect the rights of others into a logical and coherent system of fundamental rights. He claims that this system contributed to the development of modern declarations of human rights.

107   Landman, Leo. "Law and Conscience: The Jewish View." *Judaism* 18 (1969): 17-29.

Landman discusses the tension between natural law and a divine, higher, law. A well known Jewish principle claims that the Law of the Kingdom (that is, the official legislation in any particular socio-political location) is Law (that is, must be regarded equal to Jewish Torah law and given the same status as revealed legislation). While this principle might seem to give "natural law" as expressed in civil legislation priority over divine law, Landman claims otherwise. When conflict occurs between so-called "natural law" and revelation as found in the Jewish tradition, Landman suggests that such conflict invalidates the claim of the civil legislation to actually embody natural law. Only if the civil legislation is "moral," that is, if it conforms to "natural law" and does not conflict with Torah law, does the principle of The Law of the Kingdom come into play. In the case of conscientious objection to a secular war, he suggests that each individual must decide whether the particular war is moral and thus whether the rule that the Law of the Kingdom is Law actually applies. He applies traditional Jewish principles from the Talmud and rabbinic materials to modern questions. He concludes that Judaism, as represented by this classical literature, protects the right to conscience even in the case of war.

108 Levin, Stanley. "Due Process in Rabbinical and Israeli Law: Abuse and Subversion." In *Jewish Law and Current Legal Problems*, ed. Nahum Rakover, 191-194. Library of Jewish Law Jerusalem: Jewish Legal Heritage Society, 1984.

The author suggests that every legal system has the need to prevent its abuse and subversion against citizens. The author compares Israeli law and rabbinic law in their protection against legal abuses.

109 Levinas, Emmanuel. "En Exclusivité." In his *Difficile Liberté: Essais sur le Judaisme*, 309-312. Paris: Albin Michel, 1963. French.

Levinas argues that despite apparent particularism Judaism still emphasizes the ideal of a humanity united by fraternal bonds. Prophetic universalism dies when Jews make compromises to modernity in the name of universal rights. See the translation by Sean Hand in *Difficult Freedom: Essays on Judaism*. Baltimore: Johns Hopkins University Press, 1990, 239-241.

110 Levy, Annette. "Les Droits de la Femme dans la Tradition Juive." In *Judaisme et Droits de l'Homme*, ed. Emmanuel Hirsch, 53-58. Idéologies et Droits de l'Homme B.01. Paris: Librairie des Libertés, 1984. French.

Levy contends that Jewish tradition honors women and gives them their full rights. She recalls that Genesis 1 portrays humanity as originally androgynous — a portrait implying the equality of males and females. She focuses on stories of Hebrew matriarchs and heroic women, rabbinic laws intended to improve the condition of women, and the view that no man is whole until married.

111 Lew, M. S. *Jews and Human Rights*. Jewish Topics of Today 11. London: World Jewish Congress, 1968.

The author offers a brief look at the modern discussion of human rights and the Universal Declaration of Human Rights in particular followed by a summary of the general meaning and specifically Jewish relevance of such terms as equality, unity, education, peace, justice, physical welfare, and independence. The tone is more devotional than analytic. The author concludes with the words of the rabbinic sage Hillel: that which is hateful unto you, do not do unto others.

112   Macintyre, Alasdair. "Some Consequences of the Failure of the Enlightenment Project." In his *After Virtue: A Study in Moral Theory*, 62-78. South Bend, IN: Notre Dame University Press, 1984.

In the midst of studying the consequences of the failure of a morality focused on the individual moral agent, Macintyre notes the problems inherent in a philosophy of human rights. He suggests that the lack of the concept in Hebrew, Greek, Latin or Arabic points to a plain truth: there are no such rights. Rights are fictions of moralists. This approach draws on biblical and later Jewish thinking as the source for a philosophy that denies the reality of any unalienable natural rights.

113   Meislin, B. J. "Refusal to Testify as a Protected First Amendment Religious Right." *Jewish Law Annual* 1 (1978): 219-221

After reviewing the case of a rabbi who refuses to testify on the grounds of freedom of speech, Meislin reviews Jewish law. He contends that both rabbinic teachings and philosophical principles emphasize that the imperative to testify outweighs other considerations.

114   Minogue, K. R. "Natural Rights, Ideology, and the Game of Life." In *Human Rights*, eds. Eugene Kamenka and Alice Erh-Soon Tay, 13-35. London: Edward Arnold, 1978.

Minogue begins with Karl Marx's rejection of a theory of natural rights as expressed in his 'On the Jewish Question.' He then suggests that all idéologies are hostile to the idea of natural rights. He compares theories of rights that imply duties, using as his example the biblical Ten Commandments, to rights that do not involve duties, focusing on the Hobbesian state of nature. Minogue concludes by agreeing with Marx that a theory of natural rights reflects human conflict but disagrees by attributing that theory to human gaming.

115   Muskat, Marion. "Judaisme et la 'Troisieme Generation' des Droits." In *Judaisme et Droits de l'Homme*, ed. Emmanuel Hirsch, 207-214. Idéologies et Droits de l'Homme   B.01. Paris: Librairie des Libertés, 1984. French.

After three generations of seeking to ensure human rights, the contemporary world displays violence and violation of those rights. Despite some biblical precedent toward the use of force such as the commandment to exterminate Amalekites, the Bible, in general, gives an example of how law and not violence should rule social life.

116 Nahmani, Hayim Simha. *Human Rights in the Old Testament*. Tel Aviv: Joseph Chachik, 1964.

Nahmani reviews the development of a modern theory of human rights and applies it to the data of the Bible. One section of his work focuses on topical concerns for rights involving land, animals, persons, and equality, independence, and freedom. The second section looks at the institutions of ancient Israel in comparison with those of the United States today.

117 Polish, Daniel F. "Judaism and Human Rights." In *Human Rights in Religious Traditions*, ed. Arlene Swidler, 40-50. New York: Pilgrim, 1982.

Drawing on rabbinic and biblical sources, Polish argues that while lacking the juridic term 'human rights,' Judaism stresses the importance of human life, dignity, and freedom. He focuses attention on Jewish practices toward slaves, ambivalence toward monarchy, and judicial process. He suggests how Jewish holidays symbolize freedom and equality.

118 Rabinowitz, Louis. "The Rights of the Individual (a response to Aharon Lichtenstein)." *Congress Monthly* 45, 3 (1978): 8-9.

The author claims that the Noachide laws express a view of human responsibility close to that indicated in the theory of human rights. The various biblical and rabbinic teachings about such laws show that classical Jewish sources envision certain rights that appertain to all humanity. The principle of service to God, for example, creates a sense of human equality indispensable for a theory of rights. In this case rights are based on divine expectations which presuppose them as the framework within which humanity can fulfill is true tasks.

119 Rackman, Emanuel. "A God Centered Humanism." In his *One Man's Judaism*, 149-171. New York: Philosophical Library, 1971.

Rackman surveys the values of Judaism and emphasizes that Jewish belief upholds the value and importance of the individual human being. He notes that Thomas Paine used biblical texts to support his claim of human equality. He argues that religious experience verifies the modern intuition granting human beings equality.

120 Rackman, Emanuel. "Judaism and Equality." In his *One Man's Judaism*, 120-145. New York: Philosophical Library, 1971.

Rackman conjectures the existence of a tension between natural inequalities and legal equalities among people. He roots the idea of equality in the idea that each person mirrors the image of God in a unique way. He applies this idea to family law, the law of slaves, and the distinction between Jew and non-Jew. He argues that equality served as a goal for society, not a putative natural right in Jewish thought. This essay is reproduced in entry 012, 33-54.

121   Rackman, Emanuel. "Talmudic Insights on Human Rights." *Judaism* 1 (1952): 158-162.

Using rabbinic texts as the basis for his claims, Rackman argues that Jewish law preserves an individual's right to dissent, to be judged by a fair legal system, to work, to be free from self-incrimination, and to freedom of religion. He insists that Judaism respects the independence of the human will.

122   Rosen-Zvi, Ariel. "The Place of the Woman in the Family in Jewish Law." In *Human Rights in Israel: Articles in Memory of Judge Haman Shelah*, ed. Ann Swersky, 109-151. Tel Aviv: Edanim and Yediot Aharonot, 1988. Hebrew.

The author reviews traditional Jewish law and lore concerning women from the biblical tale of Eve through rabbinic materials. Context and social reasons shape Jewish teachings about the place of women, not metaphysical considerations. While in theory Jewish law grants men and women similar rights, in practice the law allows existing conditions to determine the priority of men. Women and wives are often exalted in Jewish literature. Nevertheless in laws of possession and inheritance women are under the guidance of men. The limiting of rights is legitimated on social and communal grounds. Modern families, however, have established a different reality and no longer exemplify the presuppositions of traditional Jewish law. The problems associated with women's demands for recognition of their rights are evident in various conflicts occurring in modern Israel. During the pre-State period the demand for enfranchising women as voters produced controversy. The new social and economic structure of Israel raised issues such as women learning and teaching traditional Jewish texts and working outside of the home. The duties of a wife to a husband are not static ones and have changed as social contexts altered. The continuance of traditional laws of divorce exemplify one continuing problem as women seek to increase their independence and rights.

123   Rosner, Fred. "The Jewish Attitude Toward Euthanasia." In *Jewish Bioethics*, eds. Fred Rosner and J. David Bleich, 255-265. David M. L. Olivestone, series ed., Sanhedrin Jewish Studies. New York: Sanhedrin, 1979.

Rosner notes the various traditional concerns towards euthanasia as well as the difficulty of drawing a line to determine when care is no longer useful.   He reviews the classical Jewish texts from the Talmud which illuminate this issue and the relevant biblical material. This essay, as in other such entries, implicitly raises the question of a putative right to a dignified death.

124   Roth, Sol. *Halakhah and Politics: The Jewish Idea of the State*. Norman Lamm, series ed., The Library of Jewish Law and Ethics   14. Hoboken, NJ: Ktav, 1988.
This collection reproduces several articles concerning justice, equality, and human rights as understood from the sources of Jewish tradition.   Taken collectively the volume is a theoretical statement that Jewish law provides a mechanism by which personal rights and communal rights are reconciled in a system of divinely given duties. See entries 283, 284.

125   Rouner, S. Leroy. "Introduction." In *Human Rights and World's Religions*, ed. Leroy S. Rouner, 1-14.   Leroy S. Rouner, series ed., Boston University Studies in Philosophy and Religion 9. South Bend, IN: University of Notre Dame Press, 1988.

This introduction not only summarizes the major articles but places them in a general context.   Rouner suggests that the volume begins by focusing on Judaism since Muslim and Christian views of human rights are both rooted in the religion of Israel. He notes that ancient Israel regarded all persons as bearers of inalienable human rights. He claims that virtually all the essays, including the one on Judaism, criticize the Western, secular, notion of universal human rights.

126   Sarna, Nahum M. *The JPS Torah Commentary: Genesis*.   Philadelphia: Jewish Publication Society, 1989.

Sarna comments on the well known story of Sodom and suggests that the point of the story is moral sin, not cultic or ritual error.   The Sodomites offend against a universal moral code, they infringe on universal human rights, and are therefore punished.   Sarna implies that this view of a universal human code represents a distinctive Jewish approach to rights and duties.

127   Shapira, Amos. "Human Right to Die: Israeli and Jewish Legal Perspectives." *Israel Yearbook on Human Rights* 7 (1977): 127-138.

Shapira reviews cases in Israel regarding euthanasia and suicide. He then studies the rabbinic and biblical sources that could guide a decision in those cases and suggests that since the tradition considers pain an excuse in the case of suicide it might be permitted. This essay is also found in *The Dying Human*, eds. Andre de Vries and Amnon Carmi, 359-371, Tel Aviv: Turtledove, 1979.

128   Sherwin, Byron L. "Health, Healing and Tradition." In his *In Partnership with God: Contemporary Jewish Law and Ethics*, 66-84. Syracuse: Syracuse University Press, 1990.

Sherwin shows how concern for human rights necessitates concern for the health of every person. He points to biblical and rabbinic material that support this view. According to Judaism, the right to medical care derives from the image of God stamped upon every human being.

129   Sherwin, Byron L. "Jewish Views on Euthanasia." *Humanist* 34, 4 (1974): 19-21.

Sherwin declares that the Jewish view is not as straightforward as usually thought. He gives a careful study that shows how even active euthanasia may at times be acceptable in Jewish thinking.

130   Sherwin, Byron L. "The Sanctity of Life in an Age of Violence." In his *In Partnership with God: Contemporary Jewish Law and Ethics*, 169-180. Syracuse: Syracuse University Press, 1990.

Sherwin reviews the Jewish ideas of holiness, of personal uniqueness, and the image of God that every person shares. He supports his contentions with citations from the Hebrew Bible and rabbinic sources, showing how the Jewish vision of human value, rooted in consciousness of the divinity, counteracts the violence of modern times.

131   Sherwin, Byron L. "To Be Or...A Jewish View of Euthanasia." *United Synagogue Review* 25, 1 (1972): 4-5.

This essay summarizes traditional Jewish law and suggests three basic principles: self-destruction is also murder, no human being is an obstacle to be removed, all life is intrinsically valuable.

132   Sherwin, Byron L. "A View of Euthanasia." *Journal of Aging and Judaism* 2, 1 (1987): 35-57.

Sherwin reviews the various arguments in Jewish law concerning euthanasia and its permissibility. Not only does he look at the Bible, talmud, and medieval works but at later legal texts, particularly a nineteenth century work by Rabbi Hayyim Palaggi. Sherwin stresses the Jewish concern with the sanctity of human life and the rights of every human being including the right to terminate pain and suffering. The article is reprinted in his *In Partnership with God*, pp. 85-101.

133   Shestack, Jerome J. "The Jurisprudence of Human Rights." In *Human Rights in International Law: Legal and Policy Issues*, ed. Theodor Meron, 71-113. Oxford: Clarendon, 1984.

The author summarizes the major trends in thinking about human rights. Among other theories, he examines the theological approached based on the biblical tradition and the Marxian tradition following Marx's critique of the Jewish demand for human rights.

134   Silver, Daniel Jeremy. "The Right to Die." In *Jewish Reflections on Death*, ed. Jack Reimer, 117-125. New York: Schocken, 1975.

Silver reviews the differing attitudes of the Jewish tradition on the appropriateness of interfering with the natural process. He shows how biblical and rabbinic literature address the "right to life" and its significance. He concludes by suggestion his own view which is that life is more than mere biological functioning.

135   Strauss, Leo. *Natural Right and History.* Chicago: University of Chicago Press, 1957.

Strauss argues that biblical religion is by its very essence opposed to a theory of rights, being founded on revelation. He traces the transition from an emphasis on natural duties to modern individualism and an emphasis on natural rights. This controversial book stimulated both Jewish and general discussion.

136   Strauss, Leo, and Joseph Cropsey. "Introduction." In *History of Political Philosophy*, eds. Leo Strauss and Joseph Cropsey, 1-6. Chicago: University of Chicago Press, 1987.

> The ideas expressed here are those of Strauss who argues that political philosophy begins with the concept of "nature" in contrast to "convention." Natural rights, understood this way, cannot be the product of religious thinking but only of political philosophy. The article interprets classical Jewish texts such as the Bible no less than philosophical texts.

137   Urian, Meir. "Civil Liberty and Freedom of Expression." In his *In the Circle of Hassidism and in the Paths of Our Time*, 250-254. Jerusalem: Rubin Mass, 1977. Hebrew.

> Drawing on an analysis of the creation story and Adam's expulsion from Eden, Urian argues for the need to balance human initiative with restrictions on pursuit of personal self-interest. He takes the case of the tension between the need for free expression of ideas and the need for social control of certain ideas as his primary example. He recalls a movie concerning Arab persecution of Jews in Iraq shown to immigrants from Kurdistan. Given their background and situation, he claims, the movie could only inflame their hatred of Arabs and lead them to act against the closest target they could find, their own neighbors, the Israeli Arabs. They needed to have their fires quenched, but instead they were given a box of matches! He concludes that the social good may require censorship of the media.

138   Walzer, Michael. "Free Time." In his *Spheres of Justice: A Defense of Pluralism and Equality*, 184-196. New York: Basic Books, 1983.

> Using the Sabbath as an example, Walzer shows that leisure is not merely the absence of work but the freedom to choose what one does. He rejects, however, the idea that vacations are part of a list of human rights. Since free time has no single meaning, the structure of its allocation must differ from culture to culture. The right which Walzer affirms is that of being included in the type of use of leisure central to the culture in which one shares.

139   Walzer, Michael. *Spheres of Justice: A Defense of Pluralism and Equality*. New York: Basic Books, 1983.

> In the preface to this suggestive and penetrating study Walzer notes that the concept of equality needs interpretation. He recognizes that his interpretation is radically particularist, and in his case that particularism includes a Jewish orientation that draws on biblical sources. He explicitly rejects a general theory of natural rights since

such an approach multiplies claims to universal rights to an absurd extreme. Despite this rejection, however, several of the chapters in the book include reflections on Jewish sources and the idea of human rights.

140　Weiler, Gershon. "On Freedom of Religion and Worship." In *Human Rights in Israel: Articles in Memory of Judge Haman Shelah*, ed. Ann Swersky, 22-35. Tel Aviv: Edanim and Yediot Aharonot, 1988. Hebrew.

The author notes that the idea of a theocracy is Jewish but that it reaches a caricature in fundamentalist Islam. Although the interaction of religion and the state might appear to be born of Judaism, it actually finds its origins in the first reflective philosophy--that of Plato. Weiler notes the difference between the Jewish view of the legitimacy of the state and that which developed in Christianity and the difference between European and English approaches to the state. In modern Israel, he claims, the Israeli nation lives under the domination of an alien power -- traditional Judaism. Freedom of religion and worship for communities is not enough to ensure human rights--the individual has a right to freedom from the bondage of traditional communities, the right to set their own goals and priorities. Weiler criticizes religious parties in Israel for preventing the realization of such freedom.

141　Weiler, Gershon. "Rights of Man and Visions of Man." *Israel Yearbook on Human Rights* 12 (1982): 157-175.

Weiler contrasts Kant's theory of rights to the theory of divine commandments enunciated by the medieval Jewish philosopher Maimonides. In contrast to Kant, Maimonides accepts no autonomy and consistently claims that it is impossible. Weiler contends that in Judaism rights are expressed as the result of duties and that the latter are primary.

142　Williams, John. "The Churches, the Noahite Covenant, and Anti-Semitism." In *Anti-Semitism and Human Rights*, ed. Serge Liberman, 107-113. North Melbourne, Vic.: Australian Institute of Jewish Affairs, 1985.

Looking at biblical ethics, the author claims that at times the acceptance of injustice is itself injustice. The failure of Christians to defend human rights, he thinks, may be explainable by a failure to observe the first of the Noahite laws--that of rejecting idolatry.

143　Wyschogrod, Michael. "Judaism and Conscience." In *Standing Before God: Studies on Prayer in Scriptures and in Tradition with Essays in*

Honor of John M. Oesterreicher, eds. Asher Finkel and Lawrence Frizzell, 313-328. New York: Ktav, 1981.

Wyschogrod notes that the danger of conscience lies in its autonomy which conflicts with the biblical ethics of obedience. He provides a persuasive explanation of how the Hebrew Bible directs action without specific reference to conscience. When conscience and law conflict, one must choose conscience. He solves the problem by suggesting that while the right to follow an unerring conscience is immutable, the test of such a conscience lies in keeping it sensitive to Torah and the divine commandments. No one is guilty for following conscience, but may be guilty for not having a conscience that perceives the voice what God actually demands.

144   Wyschogrod, Michael. "Religion and International Human Rights: A Jewish Perspective." In *Formation of Social Policy in the Catholic and Jewish Traditions*, eds. Eugene J. Fisher and Daniel F. Polish, 123-141. South Bend, IN: University of Notre Dame Press, 1980.

Wyschogrod provides biblical and talmudic sources to show the values of Judaism and their relevance to human rights. He suggests that the failure to honor human rights often precedes and anticipates atrocities against a nation's population.

145   Zeltner, Zeev. "Human Rights Considered as Religious Rights." *Tel Aviv University Law Review (Iyyunei Mishpat)* 3, 1 (1978): 5-13.

The author argues that the rabbinic story in which the majority opinion outweighs the divine shows the importance of freedom of conscience. Thus respect for rights is motivated by religious rather than merely economic or philosophical reasons. He compares Jewish views of rights to those expressed by the Chinese, Hindu, and Muslim traditions and concludes that the Western understanding of rights from Thomas Paine through Thomas Mann reflects the Judaic approach.

146   Zeltner, Zeev. "The Struggle for Human Rights and Its Implications." In
      Of Law and Man: Essays in Honor of Haim Cohn, ed. Shlomo
      Shoham, 47-57. New York: Sabra, 1971.

      Zeltner claims the Hebrew prophets intertwined the love of peace
      and the affirmation of human rights. Ultimately all modern views
      of human rights trace their roots to the Hebrew Bible. All modern
      views, however, are not equally biblical. Comparing the prophetic
      view of human rights to views found in Western culture generally,
      in Marxist countries, and among the Arab states, he concludes that
      using the same term in each case is misleading.

3

Jewish Theories
of Human Rights

147   Agi, Marc. "Judaisme et Droits de l'Homme." In *Judaisme et Droits de l'Homme*, ed. Emmanuel Hirsch, 3-21. Idéologies et Droits de l'Homme B.01. Paris: Librairie des Libertés, 1984. French.

> See the annotation at entry 041.

148   Agi, Marc. *René Cassin: Fantassin des Droits de l'Homme*. Paris: Plon, 1979. French.

> More than a mere biography, this study of René Cassin, winner of the Nobel Prize in 1968, traces his involvement in issues of human rights from his youth in France through his response to World War II and its aftermath and shows how Cassin's actions follow his conviction that "it is impossible to separate the emancipation and defense of Jews from that of all other human beings." The book helps explain Cassin's understanding of the State of Israel as a means for ensuring that Jews enjoy human rights. Cassin's ability to trace the "partial victories" in the struggle for human rights from the French Revolution until modern times helps place both the specifically Jewish and generally human understanding of this concept into perspective. It shows how awareness of antisemitism leads to consciousness of any threat to human rights. Until his death in 1976 Cassin argued that Judaism gave human civilization the lesson of the dignity every human being. While a devotional biography, this book informs readers of how one prominent Jew saw the interplay between his religious tradition and the idea of human rights.

149   Agus, Irving A. "The Rights and Immunities of the Minority." *Jewish Quarterly Review*, n.s, 45 (1954-55): 120-129.

> Agus studies how Jewish law protects the rights of minorities. He notes that community depends upon voluntary consent for the restriction of freedoms. Such restrictions do not violate human rights because they depend on a freely given acceptance of their power.

150   Agus, Jacob B. "Religious Liberty in Judaism." In *Religious Liberty and Human Rights in Nations and in Religions*, ed. Leonard Swidler, 167-174. Philadelphia and New York: Ecumenical Press and Hippocrene Books, 1986.

Agus shows how Jewish thinking on human rights arises from the modern and contemporary Jewish experience.   While the early moderns emphasized freedom of conscience and the Jewish recognition of differing views, post-Holocaust Jews recognize that the right to survival depends upon communal loyalty.   Thus he contrasts Moses Mendelssohn's view that religion expresses individual conscience to the Zionist view that emphasizes nationalism and the creation of a messianic community.   He sees the two as representing a polarity of freedom and law in Jewish life and traces this polarity through Jewish history.

151   Agus, Jacob B. *The Vision and the Way : An Interpretation of Jewish Ethics*. New York: Frederick Ungar, 1966.

Agus defines human rights as the conditions necessary for a person to become most fully human.   He locates the concern with such rights in American Jewish society and shows its relevance to Jewish ethics generally.

152   Altmann, Alexander. "Moses Mendelssohn as the Archetypal German Jew." In *The Jewish Response to German Culture From the Enlightenment to the Second World War*, eds. Jehuda Reinharz and Walter Schatzberg, 17-31. Hanover, NH: University Press of New England, 1985.

Pointing to the ways in which Mendelssohn's example stood as an ideal which German Jews imitated, Altmann shows how his agenda of human rights became that of Gabriel Reisser.   Mendelssohn's belief in human rights explains why he sought a political rather than social solution to what became known as the 'Jewish Question.' Mendelssohn represents a legalistic view of rights in contrast to the view that Jews require rehabilitation before becoming eligible for rights.

153   Andrew, Edward. *Shylock's Rights: A Grammar of Lockian Rights*. Toronto: University Press of Toronto Press, 1988.

Andrew argues that the language of rights exists because of social conflict and antagonism.   He surveys philosophers of rights from Hobbes through modern theorists such as Robert Nozick.   He refers frequently to antisemitism as a test case not only in Shakespeare and Locke but also in Burke, Marx, and modern cases in which

Nazi-sympathizers have been prosecuted.   He concludes that the language of rights will be unnecessary when society has been transformed.

154   Aschheim, Steven E. "Jew Within: The Myth of 'Judaization' in Germany." In *The Jewish Response to German Culture From the Enlightenment to the Second World War*, eds. Jehuda Reinharz and Walter Schatzberg, 212-241. Hanover, NH: University Press of New England, 1985.

Aschheim traces the history of the claim that Jews have corrupted German culture and includes references to Bruno Bauer's tract on Jewish civil rights as well as Karl Marx's response to that tract. He judges Marx's support for such rights 'ambiguous in the extreme' and considers Marx's writing a continuing antisemitic element in Socialism.

155   Atlas, Samuel. "Rights of Private Property and Private Profit." *Central Conference of American Rabbis Yearbook* 54 (1944): 212-256.

Although focused on economic concerns this essay emphasizes the theory of rights in Judaism. Atlas notes that, like Locke, Jewish law makes labor, not occupancy, the basis for the right to ownership. He notes the limitations imposed on individuals not to enslave themselves and remarks that duties, in Judaism, may often supersede rights.

156   Avineri, Shlomo. "Marx and Jewish Emancipation." *Journal of the History of Ideas* 25 (1964): 445-450.

Avineri focuses on Marx's revision of his view of the Jewish Question in his contributions to *The Holy Family* and suggests that Marx defended the right of the Jews to emancipation while still opposing their role in the social and political system into which they were being emancipated.   He recognizes that this view of antisemitism and its relationship to emancipation springs from Marx's general approach to human rights.

157   Bamberger, Bernard. "Individual Rights and the Demands of the State: The Position of Classical Judaism." *Central Conference of American Rabbis Yearbook* 54 (1955): 197-212.

See the annotation at entry 043.

158   Bar Navi, Eli. "Civil Rights--a Historical Perspective." In *Human Rights in Israel: Articles in Memory of Judge Haman Shelah*, ed. Ann Swersky, 11-21. Tel Aviv: Edanim and Yediot Aharonot, 1988. Hebrew.

See the annotation at entry 044.

159   Barnet, Kriegel Blandine. "Judaisme et Droit de l'Homme." In *Judaisme et Droits de l'Homme*, ed. Emmanuel Hirsch, 127-131. Idéologies et Droits de l'Homme Paris: Librairie des Libertés, 1984. French.

See the annotation at entry 047.

160   Baron, Salo W. "The Evolution of Equal Rights: Civil and Political." *Essays on Human Rights: Contemporary Issues and Jewish Perspectives*, eds. David Sidorsky, *et al.*, 267-281. Philadelphia: Jewish Publication Society, 1979.

Baron emphasizes the distinction between civil and political rights. Thus many Jews feared political emancipation. He shows how the granting of political rights often had little effect on either the political life of the community as a whole or on the economic life of Jews in particular.

161   Baron, Salo Wittmayer. *The Russian Jew Under Tsars and Soviets*. New York: Macmillan, 1976.

Throughout, Baron shows how Russian Jews championed the ideal of universal human rights seeking to gain their own civil liberties. He notes that the pattern of reform followed by reversals which began in Tsarist Russia continued under the Soviets. Baron believes that the granting of Jewish rights and human rights are interlinked and narrates approvingly of Paul Robeson's affirming of the Jewish struggle of such rights. He also notes, however, the division among Russian Jews over whether they should fight for such rights in Russia or seek freedom through emigration. Thus he considers how Jewish thought itself emphasizes the importance of equal rights as an ideal.

162   Baruk, Henri. "Droits et Devoirs Dan La Tradition Hebraique." In *Judaisme et Droits de l'Homme*, ed. Emmanuel Hirsch, 23-38. Idéologies et Droits de l'Homme Paris: Librairie des Libertés, 1984. French.

      See the annotation at entry 048.

163   Beame, Abraham D. "Liberalism." *Judaism* (1972): 36-38.

      Beame argues that the Jewish tradition supports liberalism as a means of ensuring the protection of minority rights.

164   Belkin, Samuel. *In His Image: The Jewish Philosophy of Man as Expressed in Rabbinic Tradition*. Westport, CT: Greenwood, 1979.

      See the annotation at entry 051.

165   Belkin, Samuel. "The Sacredness of Human Life." In his *In His Image: The Jewish Philosophy of Man as Expressed in Rabbinic Tradition*, 97-116. Westport, CT: Greenwood, 1979.

      See the annotation at entry 053.

166   Ben-Gal, Teli. *The Right to Equality*. Jerusalem: The Association for Civil Rights in Israel, 1990. Hebrew.

      The editor has created a valuable workbook filled with readings on the rights of citizens in Israel. The material includes reflections on Jewish sources for defining human rights, the right to equal treatment, and the practice of such rights in the State of Israel.

167   Ben-Gal, Teli and Zoref, Zivka, eds. *Civil Rights in Israel*. Jerusalem: The Association for Civil Rights in Israel, 1988. Hebrew.

      This experimental edition of a workbook for teaching about rights in public schools includes theoretical considerations of the historical development of a theory of rights, international conventions concerning rights and equalities, and practical examination of incidents in Israel.

168   Bialik, Hayym Nahman. *Divrei Sifrut (Literary Essays)*. Tel Aviv: Devir, 1964. Hebrew.

      Several of Bialik's essays here, especially "The Hebrew Book," pp. 25-41 and "The Science of Judaism," pp. 87-94, contrast the Western Jew's search for equal rights of citizenship with the true rights of a nation to its own language and culture. See the English translation of the first essay by Minnie Halkin, *The Hebrew Book: An Essay*. Jerusalem: Bialik Institute, 1952.

169   Bick, Etta, ed. "Darchei Shalom." In her *Judaic Sources of Human Rights*, 45-87. Tel Aviv: Israel-Diaspora Institute, 1987.

See the annotation at entry 002.

170   Bick, Etta, ed. *Judaic Sources of Human Rights*. Tel Aviv: Israel-Diaspora Institute, 1987.

See the annotation at entry 003.

171   Bick, Etta, ed. "Pekuah Nefesh." In her *Judaic Sources of Human Rights*, 99-114. Tel Aviv: Israel-Diaspora Institute, 1987.

See the annotation at entry 004.

172   Bick, Etta, ed. "Sheat Hadechak." In her *Judaic Sources of Human Rights*, 16-44. Tel Aviv: Israel-Diaspora Institute, 1987.

The participants in the discussion discuss the principle of the necessitation of time and place. Some note that the members of their congregations want to respect the principles of Judaism and be able to find the concepts of freedom of conscience, democracy, and individualism in Jewish law. They debate the relationship of legal and extra-legal considerations in making decisions about Jewish practice. The role of modern experience in defining human rights becomes clear in this discussion.

173   Blaustein, Albert. "Contemporary Trends in Constitution - Writing." In *Constitutionalism: The Israeli and American Experiences*, ed. Daniel J. Elazar, 171-177. Lanham, MD: University Press of America, 1990.

See the annotation at entry 056.

174   Bleich, J. David. "Judaism and Natural Law." *Jewish Law Annual* 7 (1988): 5-42.

See the annotation at entry 057.

175   Blidstein, Gerald J. "Moral Generalizations and Halakhic Discourse."
      S'vara: A Journal of Philosophy and Judaism 1, 2 (1991): 8-12.

      While not specifically focused on the question of human rights, this
      essay surveys how general principles such as the primacy of human
      life, the importance of human dignity, and the love of the neighbor
      function in Jewish law.   Blidstein concludes that while such
      generalizations have little effect on specific legal decisions they are
      important guides as human beings respond to challenges, problems,
      and opportunities which may not be normative in a legal sense but
      do require human decisions.   The same argument holds for the
      development of a theory of human rights.

176   Bokser, Ben Zion. "Democratic Aspirations in Talmudic Judaism." In
      Judaism and Human Rights, ed. Milton R. Konvitz, 145-155. New
      York: W. W. Norton, 1972.

      See the annotation at entry 058.

177   Borochov, Ber. "Facing Reality." In his *Nationalism and the Class
      Struggle: A Marxian Approach to the Jewish Problem, Selected
      Writings by Ber Borochov*, 89-93. New York: Young Poalei Zion
      Alliance of America, 1937.

      Borochov questions the Enlightenment rationale of rights as the basis
      for Jewish emancipation.   He advocates that Jews 'create facts'
      which alone can bring equal rights. He claims that only an oppressed
      people's actions can liberated it, not reliance on general
      philosophical notions.

178   Borowitz, Eugene B. *Exploring Jewish Ethics: Papers on Covenant
      Responsibility*. Detroit, MI: Wayne State University Press, 1990.

      This collection of articles, many of which appeared previously,
      includes several essays on subjects of human rights in Judaism.

179   Borowitz, Eugene B. "Freedom: The Metamorphoses of a Jewish Value."
      In his *Exploring Jewish Ethics: Papers on Covenant Responsibility*,
      289-294. Detroit, MI: Wayne State University Press, 1990.

      When describing the modern period, Borowitz suggests how the term
      emancipation changed from meaning the formal process of freeing
      a slave to meaning enfranchising previously excluded populations of
      a citizenry. He also emphasizes that modern Jews refuse to abandon
      this idea despite the problem its attendant concept of autonomy
      brings with it.

180   Borowitz, Eugene B. "Rethinking the Reform Jewish Theory of Social Action." *Journal of Reform Judaism* 27 (1980): 1-19.

Borowitz notes the tension between Judaism's duty-oriented approach and the universalism of modern ethics. He remarks that concern for humankind, out of which the idea of universal human rights arose, represents a peculiarly modern perspective that often fails to protect any specific group, and particularly Jews. This essay is reproduced in his *Exploring Jewish Ethics* (entry 178) pp. 359-374.

181   Borowitz, Eugene B. "The Torah, Written and Oral, and Human Rights: Foundations and Deficiencies." In *The Ethics of World Religions and Human Rights*, eds. Hans Küng and Jürgen Moltmann, 25-33. London: SCM, 1990.

See the annotation at entry 061.

182   Bracha, Baruch. "Personal Status of Persons Belonging to No Recognized Religious Community." *Israel Yearbook on Human Rights* 5 (1975): 88-119.

The author asks whether personal law may be considered as an individual's religious law and answers in the negative. He still contends that they should have recourse to civil courts and measures. The article also considers the general claim that all persons possess rights by the mere fact of their humanity.

183   Braude, Samuel G. "Civil Disobedience and the Jewish Tradition." In *Judaism and Ethics*, ed. Daniel Jeremy Silver, 229-239. New York: Ktav, 1970.

Braude emphasizes the importance of loyalty to Judaism as the touchstone of civil disobedience. He thinks that this specific value, rather than a general theory of human rights, provides the best rationale for acting against legally enforced norms deemed unethical.

184   Brichto, Herbert Chanan. "The Bible on Human Rights." In *Essays in Human Rights: Contemporary Issues and Jewish Perspectives*, eds. David Sidorsky, *et al.*, 215-233. Philadelphia: Jewish Publication Society, 1979.

See the annotation at entry 062.

185   Brickner, Balfour. "Social Policy Making Structures and the Jewish Community." In *Formation of Social Policy in the Catholic and Jewish Traditions*, eds. Eugene J. Fisher and Daniel Polish, 5-14. South Bend, IN: University of Notre Dame Press , 1980.

This passionate defense of Jewish ethical concern suggests that Jews assume certain universal principles that apply to all human beings. This conviction, Brickner believes, produces an extensive agenda designed to preserve universal human rights for all humanity.

186   Bronsen, David. "Foreword." In *Jews and Germans From 1860-1933: The Problematic Symbiosis*, ed. David Bronsen, 1-8. Heidelberg: Carl Winter, 1979.

Bronsen traces the changes that brought Jews into the mainstream of German culture and the romanticism that undermined this attempt at integration. These changes influenced Jewish self-understanding and the interpretation of human rights within the inherited Jewish tradition. He notes that the struggle for civil rights went on for generations before a short-lived attainment in the Weimar Republic followed by their complete extinction under the Nazis.

187   Bulka, Reuven. "The Role of the Individual in Jewish Law." *Tradition* 13/14 (1973): 124-136.

Bulka emphasizes the human right to growth and psychological development. As such Jewish law, according to him, provides the basic environment needed for this right.

188   Byrd, B. Sharon. "Justice and Talionis." *S'vara: A Journal of Philosophy and Judaism* 1, 2 (1991): 65-68.

Byrd argues that both talmudic and Kantian thought are humanitarian. They both limit the state in its reaction toward a criminal offender. In this case they show a humanitarian concern for the rights of both the victim and the offender.

189   Calef, Michel. "Un Regard Juif sur l'Ambiguité des Droits de l'Homme." In *Judaisme et Droits de l'Homme*, ed. Emmanuel Hirsch, 133-160. Idéologies et Droits de l'Homme   B.01. Paris: Librairie des Libertés, 1984. French.

Judaism consists of texts, collective memory, and concrete men and women. It includes several openings and clues for the perception of human rights through the stories of creation, Noah, Abraham, and Sinai. The modern paradox lies in the homage given by vice to virtue, an idealization of the past used as a goal for the future, and a skeptical politics used as the basis for laws ensuring human rights. Jews, both because of the Nazi Holocaust and the modern State of Israel, point to a rational optimism for a progress toward human rights.

190   Carlebach, Julius. *Karl Marx and the Radical Critique of Judaism.* London: Kegan Paul, 1978.

Although focused on Marx's view of the Jews rather than on his view of human rights, this book provides substantial historical background and a sketch of Jewish responses to Bruno Bauer's criticism of the Jewish desire for emancipation. His presentation of Gabriel Riesser's defense of Jewish rights as part of universal human rights and his summary of Moses Hess's views illuminate Jewish views of human rights. The book includes a valuable annotated bibliography.

191   Carmi, Amnon. "Freedom and Human Rights." In his *On Law and Medicine*, 15-27. Haifa: Tamar, 1987.

Carmi claims that Judaism considers freedom and human rights valuable because of the unique importance given to the individual in Jewish thought. He surveys views of slaves, defective persons, children, women, and free choice and compares Jewish and non-Jewish approaches. While focused on medical issues, this essay raises general questions about the meaning of human rights in the Jewish tradition and the place of freedom among those rights.

192   Carmi, Amnon. "To Live Like A King: Die Like A King." In his *Law and Medicine*, 28-63. Haifa: Tamar, 1987

See the annotation at entry 063.

193   Carmon, Arye, Prologue. In *Judaic Sources of Human Rights*, ed. Etta Bick, vii-viii. Tel Aviv: Israel-Diaspora Institute, 1987.

Carmon explains how the question of who is a Jew raised the additional dilemma of defining a Jewish Bill of Rights for the State of Israel. Not only do the problems of legal procedure and the right to equality before the law arise from this situation, but also questions concerning the right to freedom of conscience in a Jewish state require attention. Readers will discern a concern with defining the very meaning of human rights underlying these discussions.

194   Cassin, René. "From the Ten Commandments to the Rights of Man." In *Of Law and Man: Essays in Honor of Haim Cohn*, ed. Shlomo Shoham, 13-25. New York: Sabra, 1971.

See the annotation at entry 065.

195   Cohn, Haim H. "Discrimination of Jewish Minorities in Arab Countries." *Israel Yearbook on Human Rights* 1 (1971): 127-133.

Cohn finds in Arabs a conscious or unconscious desire to take revenge against the Jews for the establishment of the State of Israel. He traces how Jewish minorities in Arab lands have lost their rights to due process, to work, to property, to education, to inherit or pass on property to descendants. He considers these problems within the framework of a general theory of human rights.

196   Cohn, Haim H. "Discriminations of Women." In his *Human Rights in Jewish Law*, 167-177. New York: Ktav, 1984.

See the annotation at entry 067.

197   Cohn, Haim H. *Human Rights in the Bible and Talmud*. Jerusalem: Ministry of Security, 1988. Hebrew.

See the annotation at entry 068.

198   Cohn, Haim H. "Introduction." In *Judaic Sources of Human Rights*, ed. Etta Bick, 1-15. Tel Aviv: Israel-Diaspora Institute, 1987.

See the annotation at entry 069.

199   Cohn, Haim H. "On the Meaning of Human Dignity." *Israel Yearbook on Human Rights* 13 (1983): 226-251.

Cohn notes that legal terminology uses 'human dignity' as a synonym for human worth and the source from which to derive human rights and liberties. Cohn argues that human dignity presupposes the equality of worth of all human beings and does not require living up to an ideal pattern. Since human life and person are inviolable, he contends, every person has the right to a dignified death. In Jewish tradition, loving the neighbor, he claims, means enabling him to have an easy death. God, Cohn learns from Jewish sources, created human death to save human dignity.

200   Cohn Haim H. *Jewish Issues at the United Nations Council on Human Rights*. Moshe Davis, series ed., Study Circle on Diaspora Jewry Series Three, no. 4. Jerusalem: The Institute of Contemporary Jewry, 1969. Hebrew.

Cohn discusses the problem of the variety of groups representing Jewish interests in Human Rights at the United Nations. He mentions the issues of the exclusion of antisemitism in the resolution against racism, of the Jews in the Soviet Union and in Argentina, and wonders whether Israel should be the official representative of the Jewish concern for human rights world wide.

201   Cropsey, Joseph. "Karl Marx." In *History of Political Philosophy*, eds. Leo Strauss and Joseph Cropsey, 802-825. Chicago: University of Chicago Press, 1987.

Cropsey makes use of Marx's thinking on human rights as expressed in "On the Jewish Question," but never considers the relationship of that thought to antisemitism or to Jews.

202   Daube, David. "The Rabbis and Philo on Human Rights." In *Human Rights in Essays on Human Rights: Contemporary Issues and Jewish Perspectives*, ed. David Sidorsky, *et al.*, 234-246. Philadelphia: Jewish Publication Society, 1979.

See the annotation at entry 071.

203   Elazar, Daniel J., ed. *Constitutionalism: The Israeli and American Experiences*. Lanham, MD: University Press of America, 1990.

See the annotation at entry 007.

204   Elazar, Daniel J. "Constitution-Making: The Pre-Eminently Political Act." In his *Constitutionalism: The Israeli and American Experiences*, 3-29. Lanham, MD: University Press of America, 1990.

Elazar traces the development of constitution-making from its beginnings in the Anglo-American tradition through the emergence of an unwritten constitution in the State of Israel. He discusses the interaction of religious concerns--such as the definition of who is a Jew and the contention that Israel's only constitution should be traditional Jewish law--and the modern concern for human rights.

205   Elazar, Daniel J. "Preface." In his *Constitutionalism: The Israeli and American Experiences*, xi-xv. Lanham, MD: University Press of America, 1990.

Elazar suggests that Israel's constitutional development exemplifies Edmund Burke's definition of the prescriptive constitution. Burke's conservatism, however, which demands rooting civil law in a higher moral law leads to a tension engendered by the theo-political aspect of the ancient constitution being adapted. He notes the conflict between such a divine constitution and that of a modern democracy committed to protecting individual rights. He notes a general agreement that Israel needs to enact a bill of rights to protect the rights of all citizens.

206   Esbeck, Carl H. *Religious Beliefs, Human Rights, and the Moral Foundation of Western Democracy: 1986 Paine Lectures.* Columbia, MO: University of Missouri-Columbia Press, 1986.

See the annotation at entry 008.

207   Falk, Zeev W. "Human Rights." In his *Law and Religion: The Jewish Experience*, 75-89. Jerusalem: Mesharim, 1981. Hebrew.

See the annotation at entry 073.

208   Falk, Zeev. "The Rights of the Individual (a response to Aharon Lichtenstein)." *Congress Monthly* 45, 3 (1978): 8.

Falk claims that Judaism is not necessarily a closed system. When understood in a dynamic and responsive way Judaism does not conflict with the idea of human rights.

209   Finkelstein, Louis. "Human Equality in the Jewish Tradition." *Conservative Judaism* 10, 1 (1955): 1-27.

See the annotation at entry 075.

210   Fishbane, Michael. "The Image of the Human and the Rights of the Individual in Jewish Tradition." In *Human Rights and World's Religions*, ed. Leroy S. Rouner, 17-32. Leroy S. Rouner, series ed., Boston University Studies in Philosophy and Religion 9. South Bend, IN: University of Notre Dame Press, 1988.

See the annotation at entry 076.

211   Fox, Marvin. "Maimonides and Aquinas on Natural Law." *Dine Israel* 3 (1973):

See the annotation at entry 077.

212   Foxman, Abraham H. "Anti-semitism in the United States." In *Anti-Semitism and Human Rights*, ed. Serge Liberman, 19-26. North Melbourne, Vic.: Australian Institute of Jewish Affairs, 1985.

While admitting that American antisemitism has been transformed and that Jews are safer in America than ever before, Foxman traces new forms of anti-Jewish activity in the United States. He suggests that the ideal of human rights has been undermined by such examples of antisemitism as that found in the United Nations and in many statements by American black leaders. He concludes that the viability of the ideal of human rights in the world will depend upon attitudes taken toward the world's smallest minority people--the Jews.

213   Garet, Ronald R. "Natural Law and Creation Stories." In *Religion, Morality, and the Law*, eds. J. Roland Pennock and John W. Chapman, 218-262. Nomos 30. New York: New York University Press, 1988.

See the annotation at entry 078.

214   Gavison, Ruth, ed. *Civil Rights in Israel*. Jerusalem: The Association for Civil Rights in Israel, 1982. Hebrew.

See the annotation at entry 009.

215   Gavison, Ruth. "The Rights to Privacy and Dignity." In *Human Rights in Israel: Articles in Memory of Judge Haman Shelah*, ed. Ann Swersky, 61-80. Tel Aviv: Edanim and Yediot Aharonot, 1988. Hebrew.

The author suggests that the idea of human dignity arises from every monotheistic faith. She considers this idea the source for every other human right. Even though these rights are not central in judicial law, they are central for both personal and communal existence. The rights of privacy are also essential to personal autonomy and human choice. She notes that technological advances create new threats to privacy and require new responses. She concludes by suggesting the challenges within the State of Israel that threaten the rights of privacy.

216   Gilman, Sander. "Karl Marx and the Secret Language of Jews." *Modern Judaism* 4, 3 (1984): 275-294.

The author examines the cultural and intellectual context in which Marx wrote on the "The Jewish Question." He shows how Marx followed Hegel's view of the Jews' right to civil emancipation and how the common antisemitic opposition to the Jews misuses the image of the Jew. He suggests that Marx associates the role of this image in society with the role of the Jews' discourse in language. He suggests that Marx is torn between models of conversion and immutability and accepts both as part of his image of Jewish nature.

217   Glatzer, Nahum N. "The Beginnings of Modern Jewish Studies." In *Studies in Nineteenth-Century Jewish Intellectual History*, ed. Alexander Altmann, 27-45. Cambridge, MA: Harvard University Press, 1964.

Despite the title of this essay which seems to focus on education, the author analyzes the way nineteenth century Jews understood their claims to deserve certain human rights. Glatzer discusses Zunz's view of universal human rights as a problematic element in his total theory. As an apologist, Zunz saw himself as the herald of a new Europe and an advocate of human rights and emancipation. At the same time, he devoted himself to construing a scheme of history to support and justify his claim for Judaism's continued relevance.

218   Goitein, S. D. "Human Rights in Jewish Thought and Life in the Middle Ages." In *Essays on Human Rights: Contemporary Issues and Jewish Perspectives*, eds. David Sidorsky, *et al.*, 247-264. Philadelphia: Jewish Publication Society, 1979.

See the annotation at entry 079.

219   Goldmann, Alain. "Les Sources Juives des Droits de l'Homme." In *Judaisme et Droits de l'Homme*, ed. Emmanuel Hirsch, 45-51. Idéologies et Droits de l'Homme   B.01. Paris: Librairie des Libertés, 1984. French.

See the annotation at entry 080.

220   Goodman, Lenn Evan. "Equality and Human Rights: The Lockean and Judaic Views." *Judaism* 25 (1967): 357-362.

Goodman traces a decline from the Jewish view of human rights rooted in the absolute worth of the human being to the Christian idea of equality in sin to the secularization of that idea in the social contract theory which grants every person the right to restrain every other one.   Equality in that case is an equal power of destructiveness. Such a view is the opposite of the Jewish view.

221   Goodman, Lenn Evan. *On Justice: An Essay in Jewish Philosophy*. New Haven: Yale University Press, 1991.

This ambitious and stimulating study draws extensively on biblical material to develop a theory of "rights" based on human capabilities. Rather than speak of rights and duties, Goodman integrates them into a single system based on "the deserts of every being in relation to the interests of all others." Goodman proceeds to apply this theory to practical cases such as those of punishment, theodicy, messianism, and human systems of justice.

222   Halpern, Ben. "Jewish Nationalism: Self-Determination as a Human Right." In *Essays on Human Rights: Contemporary Issues and Jewish Perspectives*, eds. David Sidorsky, *et al.*, 309-335. Philadelphia: Jewish Publication Society, 1979.

Halpern argues that the fundamentals of liberalism and Judaism conflict. Jewish tradition espouses a theory of collective rights, while liberalism espouses one of individual rights. Jewish advocacy for national self-determination, according to Halpern, conflicts with liberalism's championing of an international bill of rights. Liberalism finds it difficult to affirm Jewish nationalism since liberalism considers religion an inadequate basis for national identity. He comments ironically that the creation of the state of Israel did not affirm the right of a dispersed people to territorial self-determination. Nevertheless, Palestinians now recognize that principle as a basis on which to build their nationalism, but reject its application to the Jews!

223   Henkin, Louis. "Human Rights: Reappraisal and Readjustment." In *Essays on Human Rights: Contemporary Issues and Jewish Perspectives*, eds. David Sidorsky, *et al.*, 68-87. Philadelphia: Jewish Publication Society, 1979.

Henkin notes the variety of meanings implied in the term "human rights." When using the phrase Western states think of political and civil rights, Communist and Third World states of economic and social rights. Although human rights concern everyone, few nations are willing to submit to international scrutiny. Because human rights have been politicized, international concern selects only those of interest to a large constituency. Henkin argues that Jews must not allow disappointment in the human rights movement to lead to abandoning it. Diaspora and Israeli Jews, he claims, share a common concern for the preservation of universal human rights.

224   Henkin, Louis. "Judaism and Human Rights." *Judaism* 25 (1976): 357-362.

While contending that no Hebrew word corresponds to the modern idea of human rights, Henkin traces the Jewish roots of jurisprudence which support specific rights. Jewish law, however, does not provide rights against society. In Judaism rights permit the exercise of duties to God. Thus Judaism opposes libertarianism even while it exalts personal choice, human dignity, and due process of law. Even more importantly modern history shows the need for a recognized set of common human rights established in something greater than the social contract.

225 Herzog, Chaim. "Judaism, Law and Justice." *Israel Yearbook on Human Rights* 14 (1984): 9-16.

Herzog suggests that the traditional interpretation of Jewish law evolved into an expression of humanistic principles. In contrast, he claims that the United Nations is destroying the pillars of human morality. Proceedings there give evidence of fostering antisemitism and bringing discord and fanaticism. Thus law may not bring justice and the international community should look to Judaism for guidance.

226 Heschel, Abraham Joshua. *God in Search of Man: A Philosophy of Judaism*. New York: Harper and Row, 1955.

In several places in the last two thirds of this work (pp. 213-436), Heschel emphasizes that Judaism connects human dignity not just with rights but with obligations (p. 216). He claims that so-called "human rights" are not "legally protected interests of society but the sacred interests of God" (p. 288). He also avoids reification of rights and suggests, instead, that one learns about rights of others through an intense experience of ones own rights (pp. 398-399). Thus, he finally concludes, there are no independent, self-evident, rights but only rights that flow from the divine needs. The inherent worth of all things, including human beings, comes from the fact that "All is endowed with bearing on God" (p. 415). As Heschel explains it, the language of "rights" in Judaism is a metaphor for conveying divine concerns.

227 Heschel, Abraham Joshua. *The Insecurity of Freedom: Essays on Human Existence*. New York: Schocken, 1972.

See the annotation at entry 088.

228 Heschel, Abraham Joshua. "Religion in a Free Society." In his *The Insecurity of Freedom: Essays on Human Existence*, 3-23. New York: Schocken, 1972.

Heschel argues that rights must be understood in terms of human needs. He uses rabbinic sources to show that religion teaches how to transform needs into an opportunity to perceive human obligations to others.

229   Heschel, Abraham Joshua. "Sacred Image of Man." In his *The Insecurity of Freedom: Essays on Human Existence*, 150-167. New York: Schocken, 1972.

See the annotation at entry 093.

230   Hollenbach, David. "Human Rights and Religious Faith in the Middle East: Reflections of a Christian Theologian." *Human Rights Quarterly* 4, 1 (1972): 94-109.

Hollenbach surveys the way the three major religious faiths in the Middle East understand the idea of human rights. He suggests that Judaism places a greater emphasis on communal rights than on the individual. He claims that Jews insist on integrating human rights within a framework of respect for the particularities of communal identity. He considers the real task of the future to be developing an indigenous basis for pluralism.

231   Israel, Rachel. "Judaisme et Dissidence." In *Judaisme et Droits de l'Homme*, ed. Emmanuel Hirsch, 189-198. Idéologies et Droits de l'Homme B.01. Paris: Librairie des Libertés, 1984. French.

See the annotation at entry 095.

232   Israel, Richard J. "Jewish Tradition and Political Action." In *Tradition and Contemporary Experience: Essays on Jewish Thought and Life*, ed. Alfred Jospe, 189-204. New York: Schocken, 1970.

Israel notes how Jewish thought has advanced from a concern with Jewish self-preservation to a concern for rights in society as a whole. He also suggests that while Judaism demands that society honor some rights, modern western society has raised an awareness about other rights that Jews must now recognize.

233   Kamenka, Eugene. "The Anatomy of an Idea." In *Human Rights*, eds. Eugene Kamenka and Alice Erh-Soon Tay, 1-12. London: Edward Arnold, 1978.

Kamenka, using a Marxist model, traces the development of the idea of human rights. He denies that it draws exclusively on religious traditions or is a contribution of the 'Judeo-Christian' tradition. He agrees that Judaism, like Christianity and Islam, confront the mundane order with a transcendent moral system, but claims that the modern idea of universal rights represents a new and philosophical ideal.

234   Kaplan, Abraham. "Human Relations and Human Rights in Judaism." In *The Philosophy of Human Rights: International Perspectives*, ed. Alan S. Rosenbaum, 53-85. Contributions in Philosophy 15. Westwood, CT: Greenwood, 1980.

See the annotation at entry 096.

235   Kaplan, Mordecai M. *The Future of the American Jew.* New York: Macmillan, 1948.

Kaplan devotes attention to what he considers the uniqueness of the modern Jewish situation. By accepting the idea of universal human rights, Jews did what no cultural group had done before: they agreed to assimilate into one culture while retaining their own group identity. He studies the right of a cultural or religious group to function as the milieu in which the individual's rights are realized. From this perspective he evolves a set of group rights including the right to equality among religious communities and the right to diversity of expression within any religious group. See the paperback edition, New York: Reconstructionist Press, 1967.

236   Kaplan, Mordecai M. *Judaism Without Supernaturalism: The Only Alternative to Orthodoxy and Secularism.* New York: Reconstructionist, 1967.

See the annotation at entry 097.

237   Kaplan, Mordecai M. *The Meaning of God in Jewish Religion.* New York: Reconstructionist, 1962.

See the annotation at entry 098.

238   Katz, Jacob. "The Term 'Jewish Emancipation': Its Origin and Historical Impact." In *Studies in Nineteenth-Century Jewish Intellectual History*, ed., Alexander Altmann, 1-26. Cambridge, MA: Harvard University Press, 1964.

Citing its various defenders and opponents, Katz clarifies whether and to what extent the promise of the enjoyment of universal human rights was associated with the call for Jewish Emancipation. This essay includes reflections on the historical situation in which Jews found it necessary to appeal for protection of their rights. It also reviews the arguments that Jews used to show how their religion expressed the idea of human rights and what that concept entailed.

239   Kimmelman, Reuven. "Nonviolence in the Talmud." *Judaism* 17 (1968): 316-334.

    · See the annotation at entry 100.

240   Kimmelman, Reuven. "The Rabbinic Ethics of Protest." *Judaism* 19 (1970): 38-58.

    See the annotation at entry 101.

241   Kirschenbaum, Aaron. "Human Rights Revisited." *Israel Yearbook on Human Rights* 6 (1976): 228-238.

    Kirschenbaum reviews the discussion of Judaism's view of human rights. He claims that while rights protect people, duties uplift them. By insisting on human duty and asking people to go beyond their natural rights Judaism provided them with greater dignity.

242   Kirschenbaum, Aaron. "Jewish Law and the Abuse of Rights." *Tel Aviv University Studies in Law* 5 (1980/1982): 98-114.

    Kirschenbaum studies both the limitations in the restrictions on abusing recourse to law and the theoretical importance of such possibilities of abuse in Jewish, Anglo-american, and continental law. He concludes that Jewish law has stronger restrictions and seeks to enforce a moral norm: the prohibition of exercising legal rights out of selfish motivations.

243   Kohn, Eugene. "Human Rights vs. Property Rights in Jewish Law." *Reconstructionist* 1, 3 (1935): 7-14.

    Kohn begins by asserting that traditional laws need revision in the light of new situations. He then focuses on the Jewish tradition and its emphasis on human rights, especially as found in laws on property and economics. He claims that personal rights take precedence over property rights and concludes that Judaism has a positive orientation to change rather than a desire to maintain the status quo. This emphasis appears as a theory of human rights: a society must change and adapt so as to protect personal freedoms even at the expense of social rights.

244   Konvitz, Milton R. "Introduction." In his *Judaism and Human Rights*. New York: W. W. Norton, 1972.

    Konvitz admits that Hebrew has no term for human rights but claims that various biblical examples show that in concrete terms Jews have acted as if there were such rights. He sees the evolutionary spirit of

Judaism in its adaptation and transforming of values to meet new situations. He contrasts that with idolatry because it entails constant self-examination.   The Jewish theory of human rights, on this reading, consists of a flexible responsiveness which protects individual freedoms by adapting to changing situations.

245   Konvitz, Milton R. "Man's Dignity in God's World." In his *Judaism and Human Rights*, 27-32. New York: W. W. Norton, 1972.

See the annotation at entry 102.

246   Konvitz, Milton R. "Torah and Constitution : An American Bicentennial Lecture." *Proceedings of the Rabbinical Assembly* 38 (1976): 54-67.

See the annotation at entry 103.

247   Kurzweil, Zvi. "Democracy and Religious Freedom." In his *The Modern Impulse of Traditional Judaism*, 124-139. Hoboken, NJ: Ktav, 1985.

Kurzweil explores the roots of religious freedom and their relationship to democracy.   He contrasts the basic principles expressed in this social and political idea to the principles of traditional Judaism. The meaning and basis for human rights is different in Judaism than in modern democracy.

248   Landau, Lazare. "Judaisme et Droits de l'Homme." In *Judaisme et Droits de l'Homme*, ed. Emmanuel Hirsch, 59-63. Idéologies et Droits de l'Homme B.01. Paris: Librairie des Libertés, 1984. French.

See the annotation at entry 105.

249   Landau, Moshe. "The Limits of Constitutions and Judicial Review." In *Constitutionalism: The Israeli and American Experiences*, ed. Daniel J. Elazar, 197-205. Lanham, MD: University Press of America, 1990.

See the annotation at entry 106.

250   Landman, Leo. "Law and Conscience: The Jewish View." *Judaism* 18 (1969): 17-29.

See the annotation at entry 107.

251   Levin, Shamarya. *The Arena*.   Trans. Maurice Samuel, New York: Harcourt Brace; Arno, 1932; 1975.

This third volume of Levin's autobiography is framed by a discussion of rights. It begins as he leaves Germany for Russia feeling that German Jews have bartered their inalienable human right to language and identity for the civic rights of the German middle-class who embraced Enlightenment ideals. The volume ends as Levin recounts how Russian groups argued whether the most pressing issue as the Tzarist regime fell was agrarian reform or that of human equality. While the Jews, who had founded a Society for Full Rights, emphasized the latter, other Russian political groups opted for the former. Thus human rights became identified as a Jewish issue.

252   Levin, Shamarya. *Forward From Exile: The Autobiography of Shamarya Levin.* Trans. and ed. Maurice Samuel. Philadelphia: Jewish Publication Society of America, 1967.

This condensed version of the first three books of Shamarya Levin's autobiography contains much of the discussion concerning human rights and Russian Jewry found in the third volume of the four book original while omitting the discussion of the German Jewish view of rights in contrast to the Russian Jew's commitment to the fundamental right to be oneself and have one's own language and culture. This has been translated into Hebrew as *Galut VaMered: Excerpts from my Memoirs*, Tel Aviv, Dvir, 1967.

253   Levinas, Emmanuel. "En Exclusivité." In his *Difficile Liberté: Essais sur le Judaisme*, 309-312. Paris: Albin Michel, 1963. French.

See the annotation at entry 109.

254   Levinas, Emmanuel. "Nom D'Un Chien Ou Le Droit Naturel." In his *Difficile Liberté: Essais sur le Judaisme*, 187-202. Presences Du Judaisme. Paris: Albin Michel, 1963. French.

Levinas meditates on rabbinic explanation of why dogs receive meat that Jews cannot eat (Exodus 22:31) and creates a modern symbolism in which dogs symbolize how pure nature leads to rights. He records an incident in which a dog recognized the humanity of Jews interred by the Nazis even when other human beings did not. Despite his exegetical skill, he is providing a modern interpretation of tradition, not restating traditional thought. See the translation by Sean Hand in *Difficult Freedom: Essays on Judaism*. Baltimore: Johns Hopkins University Press, 1990, 151-153.

255   Levinas, Emmanuel. "Religion et Tolerance." In his *Difficile Liberté: Essais sur le Judaisme*, 225-228. Presences Du Judaisme. Paris: Albin Michel, 1963. French.

Levinas claims that despite the idea of the chosen people, Israel's intimacy with the stranger makes it a compassionate religion. Judaism turns religious absolutism into a concept of infinite responsibility. See the translation by Sean Hand in *Difficult Freedom: Essays on Judaism.* Baltimore: Johns Hopkins University Press, 1990, 172-174.

256 Lew, M. S. *Jews and Human Rights* Jewish Topics of Today 11. London: World Jewish Congress, 1968.

See the annotation at entry 111.

257 Liberman, Serge, ed. *Anti-Semitism and Human Rights.* North Melbourne, Vic.: Australian Institute of Jewish Affairs, 1985.

See the annotation at entry 013.

258 Lichtenstein, Aharon. "The Rights of the Individual: The Halakhic Perspective." *Congress Monthly* 45, 3 (1978): 4-7, 13.

Lichtenstein claims that the idea of rights is a legacy of modern Western thought since Locke, and not a traditional Jewish idea. Judaism permits only two rights: that of rejecting God's law and that of interpreting that law. The Jew is primarily a servant of the divine invested with freedom only by God. Jewish law, then, is a closed system of duties. After some discussion, Lichtenstein explains that while halakha may be compatible with a theory of human rights such a theory is still not indigenous to the halakha.

259 Low, Alfred D. *Jews in the Eyes of the Germans: From the Enlightenment to Imperial Germany.* Philadelphia: Institute for the Study of Human Issues, 1979.

Low provides a good background on how the affirmation of the rights of citizens became an increasingly unstable basis for Jewish claims in Germany. He shows how alternative Jewish responses reconceived those rights to which Jews were entitled.

260 Macintyre, Alasdair. "Some Consequences of the Failure of the Enlightenment Project." In his *After Virtue: A Study in Moral Theory*, 62-78. South Bend, IN: Notre Dame University Press, 1984.

See the annotation at entry 112.

261   Markovic, Mihailo. "Political Rights Versus Social Rights." In *Human Rights and World's Religions*, ed. Leroy S. Rouner, 46-60. Leroy S. Rouner, series ed., Boston University Studies in Philosophy and Religion 9. South Bend, IN: University of Notre Dame Press, 1988.

The unwary reader of this essay who does not know Marx's essay "On the Jewish Question" may fail to grasp the author's meaning. Although never mentioning the Jews, the distinction drawn between civil rights and human rights made in this essay draws on Marx's analysis of the Jewish desire for emancipation. He claims that political freedom and civil rights when divorced from socioeconomic rights are very limited. He contends that socioeconomic rights are legitimated not by God, by a law of nature, by a benevolent dictator, nor by liberal laws. Rather they are essential to the growth and development of any human being. They are rooted in the natural needs of every person.

262   Marx, Karl. "Die Heilige Famile." In *Historische - Kritische Gesamitausgabe*. Karl Marx and Frederick Engels, 173-388. Berlin: Marx-Engels Verlag, 1929.

In chapter six of this joint work, Marx contributes three reflective responses to Bruno Bauer on the Jewish question. These reconsiderations of the Jewish question take Gabriel Riesser's responses to Bauer as a point of departure and claim that Bauer not only mistakes political rights for human rights but also transforms every analysis into theology. He misunderstands history and historical activity by invoking the Enlightenment ideal of human rights. Rights, Marx claims, provides freedom of religion but not freedom from religion. This essay is also printed as "Die Heilige Famile." In Werke Karl Marx and Frederick Engels Vol. 2, 3-223, Berlin: Dietz, 1956. Useful translations of this essay and selections from it appear in Karl Marx, *The Early Texts*, ed. David McLellan, 131-155, New York: Oxford University Press, 1971;*The Holy Family or Critique of Critical Critique*, trans. R. Dixon, Moscow: Foreign Languages, 1956; and "A World Without Jews." Ed. Dagobert G. Runes, trans. I. Langnas, New York: The Philosophical Library, 1960.

263   Marx, Karl. "Zür Judenfrage." In *Historische-Kritische Gesamitausgabe*. Karl Marx and Frederick Engels, 576-606. Berlin: Marx-Engels Verlag, 1929.

While focused on Jews and the Jewish question, this essay contains a clear statement of Marx's considered view of the role and limitations of a theory of human rights. For Marx, rights protect the interests of a selected group within society. The idea of emancipation into human rights misses the point, he argues, since the main ideal should be emancipation from the social and economic order which makes this theory of rights necessary in the first place. The two parts of this essay combine to show how the Jewish quest for rights coincides with the rise of the middle class. The Jews become the symbol of the middle class, and antisemitism responds to the malaise caused by capitalistic society which both renders rights a necessity and ensures that the granting of political emancipation will still not liberate humanity. The essay also appears in *Werke Karl Marx and Frederick Engels*, Vol. 1, 347-377. Berlin: Dietz, 1956. See translations of this work or portions of it in Karl Marx, "Civil Liberties--the Jewish Question." Marxist Social Thought, ed. Robert Freedman, 238-251, New York: Harcourt, Brace and World, 1968; "On the Jewish Question," in *Early Writings*, trans., ed., T. B. Bottomore, 1-40, London: C.A. Watts, 1963; *Writings of the Young Marx on Philosophy and Society*, trans., ed. Lloyd Easton and Kurt H. Guddat, 216-248, Garden City, NY: Doubleday, 1967; *The Marx-Engels Reader,* ed., Robert C. Tucker, 24-51, New York: W. W. Norton, 1972; *Selected Writings* ed., David McLellan, 39-62, New York: Oxford, 1977.

264   Meron, Simha. "Freedom of Religion as Distinct from Freedom from Religion." *Israel Yearbook on Human Rights* 4 (1974): 219-240.

Meron, in contrast to Shimon Shestreet (entry 725), argues that the substance of the right to freedom of religion is more difficult to discover than that of other rights. Freedom of religion is different from freedom of conscience. While some statutes limiting these rights may be needed to preserve the rights themselves, not every case of religious or secular coercion violates human rights. He claims that, in Israel, the judiciary rarely provides relief to traditional Jews whose freedom of religion has been impaired but only to non-traditionalists.

265   Meron, Theodor. "Teaching Human Rights: An Overview." In *Human Rights in International Law: Legal and Policy Issues*, ed. Theodor Meron, 1-24. Oxford: Clarendon, 1984.

While not specifically mentioning Jews or Judaism, this introduction to a helpful volume focuses on issues such as freedom of religion and the need for a country-specific analysis of a human rights record that have important relevance for a discussion of Judaism and human rights.

266   Minogue, K. R. "Natural Rights, Ideology, and the Game of Life." In
       Human Rights, eds. Eugene Kamenka and Alice Erh-Soon Tay,
       13-35. London: Edward Arnold, 1978.

       See the annotation at entry 114.

267   Muskat, Marion. "Judaisme et la 'Troisieme Generation' des Droits." In
       Judaisme et Droits de l'Homme, ed. Emmanuel Hirsch, 207-214.
       Idéologies et Droits de l'Homme   B.01. Paris: Librairie des
       Libertés, 1984. French.

       See the annotation at entry 115.

268   Nahmani, Hayim Simha. *Human Rights in the Old Testament*. Tel Aviv:
       Joseph Chachik, 1964.

       See the annotation at entry 116.

269   Novak, David. "Natural Law, Halakhah, The Covenant." *Jewish Law
       Annual* 7 (1988): 43-67.

       Novak suggests that the idea of rights distinguishes law from ordered
       brutality. He characterizes Jewish thought as positive law rather
       than natural law since it imposes an order and rights on humanity
       through the covenantal law of God. The Torah law of the Jew, he
       claims, represents one aspect of the eternal divine law. He surveys
       the thought of major modern Jewish thinkers on the subject of Jewish
       law such as Marvin Fox and Jose Faur.

270   Peppe, Eberhard. *Marx und die Rechte der Menschen*. Berlin:
       Akaemie-Verlag, 1976. German.

       This brief survey of Marx and Engels' writings on human rights
       focuses on material in Das Kapital and the Communist Manifesto
       without a discussion of "On the Jewish Question," and so
       misrepresents the approach that Marx takes on this issue.

271   Pierson, Christopher. "Marxism and Rights." In *Approaches to Marx*, eds.
       Mark Cowling and Lawrence Wilde, 172-184. Philadelphia: Open
       University Press, 1989.

       Pierson notes that Marx considers political emancipation an advance,
       but still emphasizes the limitations of a theory based on rights.
       Jewish emancipation into citizen rights, Marx claims, is not merely
       a step to political emancipation, but the limit of that emancipation.
       True liberation requires moving beyond the dichotomy between the
       public and private self, beyond social duties and individual rights, to

fully human emancipation. Pierson criticizes this theory for limiting the value of rights to a capitalistic society which Marx considered the sole social structure to impinge on individual freedom.

272 Polish, Daniel F. "Judaism and Human Rights." In *Human Rights in Religious Traditions*, ed. Arlene Swidler, 40-50. New York: Pilgrim, 1982.

See the annotation at entry 117.

273 Pulzer, Peter. "Jewish Participation in Wilhelmine Politics." In *Jews and Germans From 1860-1933: The Problematic Symbiosis*, ed. David Bronsen, 78-99. Heidelberg: Carl Winter, 1979.

Pulzer traces Jewish liberalism from the ideology of Gabriel Riesser, whom he calls 'the intellectual father of the emancipation movement and author of the Fundamental Rights of 1848,' through Jewish participation in Wilhelmine politics. He notes that Jews shared a certain liberal way of looking at public affairs but gave little evidence of Jewish separatism or a Jewish lobby. He thereby shows that the relationship between espousing a theory of human rights and the fear of antisemitism need not also entail a relationship to a particular political agenda. He also notes that the ideal of equality in Jewish thinking, developed by Riesser, need not be rooted in Jewish tradition or theory.

274 Rabinowitz, Louis. "The Rights of the Individual (a response to Aharon Lichtenstein)." *Congress Monthly* 45, 3 (1978): 8-9.

See the annotation at entry 118.

275 Rackman, Emanuel. "A God Centered Humanism." In his *One Man's Judaism*, 149-171. New York: Philosophical Library, 1971.

See the annotation at entry 119.

276 Rackman, Emanuel. "Judaism and Equality." In his *One Man's Judaism*, 120-145. New York: Philosophical Library, 1971.

See the annotation at entry 120.

277 Rackman, Emanuel. "Talmudic Insights on Human Rights." *Judaism* 1 (1952): 158-162.

See the annotation at entry 121.

278   Reines, Chaim W. "Collectivism and Individualism in Judaism." *Judaism* 6 (1957): 240-247.

Reines argues for the rabbinic view of human dignity in contrast to the eighteenth century view of the Rights of Man. The social contract thinkers based their view of rights on a pessimistic evaluation of human nature. Reines analyzes Hermann Cohen's view of individualism and human dignity from the perspective of rabbinic Judaism.

279   Rotenstreich, Nathan. "For and Against Emancipation: The Bruno Bauer Controversy." *The Leo Baeck Institute Yearbook* 4 (1959): 3-36.

Rotenstreich reviews the various responses to Bruno Bauer's argument that Jews should not expect equal rights in German society. He notes that Bauer does not regard emancipation as a process in which the state confers rights and equality, whereas the Jewish-liberal approach represented by thinkers such as Abraham Geiger and Gabriel Riesser, argued for the inherent nature of rights. He also notes non-Jewish responses to Bauer. He gives considerable space to an analysis of Marx's view in relation to Mendelssohn's understanding of Judaism. He claims that while emancipationists legitimated the power of the state by an appeal to Natural Law, the traditional conservatives rejected Natural Law and thus Jewish emancipation.

280   Rotenstreich, Nathan. *Jew and German Philosophy: The Polemics of Emancipation*. New York: Schocken, 1984.

Rotenstreich reviews Mendelssohn's correlation of rights and duties in relationship to natural human sociability. He also notes Hermann Wagener's polemic against granting Jews citizenship on the basis of the concept of natural rights. Wagener argued that emancipation menaced Judaism by obviating Jewish uniqueness and that natural rights theory threatened the preservation of Judaism itself.

281   Rotenstreich, Nathan. "Of Rights and Duties." In his *Order and Might*, 209-222. Albany, NY: State University of New York Press, 1988.

Rotenstreich considers human rights the justifiable demands to have a place in human reality, an ensured field of activity, and an opportunity to share civilization's possessions. These demands must be justified by general principles. Rotenstreich lists principles such as justice, freedom, and equality which, in earlier chapters, he associated with Jews and Judaism. Being based on such principles, human rights are founded in transsocial and transpolitical reality even though they are formulated in socio-political terms. Human rights have no meaning unless correlated with human duties. He portrays a multilayered system of rights based on the principles justifying specific rights.

282   Roth, Sol. *Halakhah and Politics: The Jewish Idea of the State*. Norman Lamm, series ed., The Library of Jewish Law and Ethics   14. Hoboken, NJ: Ktav, 1988.

See the annotation at entry 124.

283   Roth, Sol. "Human Rights." In his *Halakhah and Politics: The Jewish Idea of the State*, 117-128.   Norman Lamm, series ed., The Library of Jewish Law and Ethics   14. Hoboken, NJ: Ktav, 1988.

Roth argues the case for an obligations oriented rather than a rights oriented position.   He notes that the covenant with Noah, the Noahide laws, obligate every person.   Because of the seven obligations on humanity as a whole, individuals have certain rights: the prohibition on murder establishes a right to life, that on theft creates a right to property, that on adultery emphasizes the right of marriage, the duty of creating courts leads to a right to justice.

284   Roth, Sol. "Individualism." In his *Halakhah and Politics: The Jewish Idea of the State*, 104-116.   Norman Lamm, series ed., The Library of Jewish Law and Ethics   14. Hoboken, NJ: Ktav, 1988.

Roth argues that Judaism does not give the individual specific rights but does demand a heroism in the fulfillment of obligations. As such the individual takes on greater value in an obligation oriented tradition than in a rights oriented one.

285   Rouner, S. Leroy. "Introduction." In *Human Rights and World's Religions*, ed. Leroy S. Rouner, 1-14.   Leroy S. Rouner, series ed.,   Boston University Studies in Philosophy and Religion   9. South Bend, IN: University of Notre Dame Press, 1988.

See the annotation at entry 125.

286   Rubinstein, Amnon. "The Struggle Over a Bill of Rights for Israel." In *Constitutionalism: The Israeli and American Experiences*, ed. Daniel J. Elazar, 139-142. Lanham, MD: University Press of America, 1990.

The author notes his objections to including a basic law that would proclaim no law discriminatory if it would be a result of Israel being either a Jewish state or the state of the Jewish people.   He argues that from both a Jewish point of view and an international legal view such a provision would be disastrous. Thus while some think that such a provision would not infringe on basic human rights, Rubenstein claims that it is incompatible with Jewish, no less than international, understanding of human rights, because he understands human rights as parts of a system that limits national values rather than one which expresses them.

287   Runes, Dagobert G., ed. *Karl Marx: A World Without Jews*. New York: The Philosophical Library, 1960.

The editor's introduction and comments stress the antisemitic quality of Marx's presentation. This introduction conveys a sense of the author's view of human rights and its contrast to Marx's. It also reveals the author's response to contemporary Marxism and its treatment of Jews. The text itself translates Marx's essays on the Jewish question and interpolates passages from the Holy Family.

288   Sarna, Nahum M. *The JPS Torah Commentary: Genesis*. Philadelphia: Jewish Publication Society, 1989.

See the annotation at entry 126.

289   Shapira, Amos. "The Israeli Supreme Court and Human Rights." In *Constitutionalism: The Israeli and American Experiences*, ed. Daniel J. Elazar, 133-137. Lanham, MD: University Press of America, 1990

The author examines how Israel's laws anchor individual rights even without a constitutional document such as a bill of rights. Israel's attention to communal consensus provides security for individual rights. Nevertheless, the author thinks a written constitution might have some advantages by explicitly articulating exceptions to basic regulations.

290   Sherwin, Byron L. "The Sanctity of Life in an Age of Violence." In his *In Partnership with God: Contemporary Jewish Law and Ethics*, 169-180. Syracuse: Syracuse University Press, 1990.

See the annotation at entry 130.

291   Shestack, Jerome J. "The Jurisprudence of Human Rights." In *Human Rights in International Law: Legal and Policy Issues*, ed. Theodor Meron, 71-113. Oxford: Clarendon, 1984.

See the annotation at entry 133.

292   Shilo, S. "Kofin Al Midat S'dom: Jewish Law's Concept of Abuse of Rights." *Tel Aviv University Law Review (Iyyunei Mishpat)* 15 (1980/82): 49-114.

Shilo argues that the abuse of rights creates problems for the judicial system as well as for judicial theory. He emphasizes the latter and compares Jewish law, Anglo-American legal systems, and continental systems of law in their orientation to the problem. Jewish law considers legal recourse a legitimate recourse to prohibit the spiteful use of the legal system itself.

293   Sirat, René-Samuel. "Preface: Droits de Dieu et Droits de l'Homme." In *Judaisme et Droits de l'Homme*, ed. Emmanuel Hirsch, xiii-xiv. Idéologies et Droits de l'Homme B.01. Paris: Librairie des Libertés, 1984. French.

See the annotation at entry 293.

294   Sorkin, David Jan. "The Invisible Community: Emancipation, Secular Culture, and Jewish Identity in the Writings of Berthold Auerbach." In *The Jewish Response to German Culture From the Enlightenment to the Second World War*, eds. Jehuda Reinharz and Walter Schatzberg, 100-119. Hanover, NH: University Press of New England, 1985.

In this essay, later incorporated in his book, Sorkin shows how Auerbach, like his contemporary Gabriel Riesser, transformed emancipation into a matter of law and universal rights. He thereupon created a Jewish subculture with particularly rich and productive fruits for German culture generally.

295   Sorkin, David Jan. *The Transformation of German Jewry, 1780-1840.* New York: Oxford University Press, 1987.

Sorkin shows how German Jewry created a subculture of its own based on a theory of natural rights that he distinguishes from the French and English theories. In Germany, as illustrated by Moses Mendelssohn and Gabriel Reisser, rights were given by the state to protect human freedom. When the optimism of this view failed, it was replaced with the theory that human rights could be granted only to those who recreated themselves through self-improvement, *Bildung*, and that the one natural right was that of self-improvement.

296   Stackhouse, Max L. *Creeds, Society, and Human Rights: A Study in Three Cultures*, 31-34. Grand Rapids, MI: Eerdmans, 1984.

The author locates 'the deepest roots of human rights' in the biblical view of life.   He regards Judaism merely as a transition to Christianity from the Hebrew Bible.   He does note that the Jews were excluded from the idealism of the French Enlightenment.   His restatement of Jewish views of human rights is overly simplistic and ignores the complex discussion within classical and modern Jewish thinking.

297   Stone, Julius. "Leeway of Choice, Natural Law and Justice in Jewish Legal Ordering." *Jewish Law Annual* 7 (1988): 210-251.

Stone summarizes the various discussions in this volume of the Jewish Law Annual.   He contends that transcendent values help protect reason from becoming blind to the ultimate vision for humanity.

298   Strauss, Leo. *Natural Right and History.* Chicago: University of Chicago Press, 1957.

See the annotation at entry 135.

299   Strauss, Leo, and Cropsey, Joseph. "Introduction." In *History of Political Philosophy*, eds. Leo Strauss and Joseph Cropsey, 1-6. Chicago: University of Chicago Press, 1987.

See the annotation at entry 136.

300   Tabory, Ephraim. "Religious Rights as a Social Problem in Israel." *Israel Yearbook on Human Rights* 11 (1981): 256-271.

Tabory discusses the conflict between individual rights, collective rights, and the public welfare in Israel.   He considers the controversies over education, legislating religious observances, archeology on suspected grave sites and their effect on Israeli life.

301   Tarcov, Nathan, and Thomas L. Pangle. "Epilogue: Leo Strauss and the History of Political Philosophy." In *History of Political Philosophy*, eds. Leo Strauss and Joseph Cropsey, 907-938. Chicago: University of Chicago Press, 1987.

The authors of this essay make clear how Strauss' experience as a Jew shaped his expression of the theory of human rights and of political philosophy generally.   They explain clearly his argument against a purely human solution to the Jewish problem and how the confusion between philosophy and religion, between Athens and Jerusalem, leads to a misunderstanding of the choices that a philosopher must make.   They show how a philosophy of human rights interacts with the social and political necessities of a modern liberal democracy.

302   Traer, Robert. "Jews." In his *Faith in Human Rights: Support in Religious Traditions for a Global Struggle*, 99-110. Washington, DC: Georgetown University Press, 1991.

Traer summarizes the major articles and essays on Judaism and human rights (using as a basis most of the material in entry 045), and the important questions concerning Israel and its relationship to the Arabs, on Soviet Jews, and on the need to establish a worldwide sensitivity to human rights after the experience of the Nazi slaughter of six million Jews.

303   Urian, Meir. "Civil Liberty and Freedom of Expression." In his *In the Circle of Hassidism and in the Paths of Our Time*, 250-254. Jerusalem: Rubin Mass, 1977. Hebrew.

See the annotation at entry 137.

304   Walzer, Michael. *Spheres of Justice: A Defense of Pluralism and Equality*. New York: Basic Books, 1983.

See the annotation at entry 139.

305   Weiler, Gershon. "On Freedom of Religion and Worship." In *Human Rights in Israel: Articles in Memory of Judge Haman Shelah*, ed. Ann Swersky, 22-35. Tel Aviv: Edanim and Yediot Aharonot, 1988. Hebrew.

See the annotation at entry 140.

306   Weiler, Gershon. "Rights of Man and Visions of Man." *Israel Yearbook on Human Rights* 12 (1982): 157-175.

See the annotation at entry 141.

307   Williams, John. "The Churches, the Noahite Covenant, and Anti-Semitism." In *Anti-Semitism and Human Rights*, ed. Serge Liberman, 107-113. North Melbourne, Vic.: Australian Institute of Jewish Affairs, 1985.

See the annotation at entry 142.

308   Wyschogrod, Michael. "Religion and International Human Rights: A Jewish Perspective." In *Formation of Social Policy in the Catholic and Jewish Traditions*, eds. Eugene J. Fisher and Daniel F. Polish, 123-141. South Bend, IN: University of Notre Dame Press, 1980.

See the annotation at entry 144.

309   Zeltner, Zeev. "Human Rights Considered as Religious Rights." *Tel Aviv University Law Review (Iyyunei Mishpat)* 3, 1 (1978): 5-13.

See the annotation at entry 145.

310   Zeltner, Zeev. "The Struggle for Human Rights and Its Implications." In *Of Law and Man: Essays in Honor of Haim Cohn*, ed. Shlomo Shoham, 47-57. New York: Sabra, 1971.

See the annotation at entry 146.

4

Judaism and Specific Human Rights

COMMUNAL RIGHTS

311 Agus, Irving A. "The Rights and Immunities of the Minority." *Jewish Quarterly Review*, n.s. 45 (1954-55): 120-129.

See the annotation at entry 149.

312 Belkin, Samuel. "The Community." In his *In His Image: The Jewish Philosophy of Man as Expressed in Rabbinic Tradition*, 117-133. Westport, CT: Greenwood, 1979.

See the annotation at entry 049.

313 Bialik, Hayym Nahman. *Divrei Sifrut (Literary Essays)*. Tel Aviv: Devir, 1964. Hebrew.

See the annotation at entry 168.

314 Bokser, Ben Zion. "Democratic Aspirations in Talmudic Judaism." In *Judaism and Human Rights*, ed. Milton R. Konvitz, 145-155. New York: W. W. Norton, 1972.

See the annotation at entry 058.

315 Borochov, Ber. "Facing Reality." In his *Nationalism and the Class Struggle: A Marxian Approach to the Jewish Problem, Selected Writings by Ber Borochov*, 89-93. New York: Young Poalei Zion Alliance of America, 1937.

See the annotation at entry 177.

316   Goitein, S. D. "Human Rights in Jewish Thought and Life in the Middle
       Ages." In *Essays on Human Rights: Contemporary Issues and Jewish
       Perspectives*, eds. David Sidorsky, *et al.*, 247-264. Philadelphia:
       Jewish Publication Society, 1979.

       See the annotation at entry 079.

317   Levin, Shamarya. *The Arena*.   Trans. Maurice Samuel, New York:
       Harcourt Brace; Arno, 1932; 1975.

       See the annotation at entry 251.

318   Liberman, Serge, ed. *Anti-Semitism and Human Rights*. North Melbourne,
       Vic.: Australian Institute of Jewish Affairs, 1985.

       See the annotation at entry 013.

FREEDOM OF CONSCIENCE

319   Agus, Jacob B. "Religious Liberty in Judaism." In *Religious Liberty and
       Human Rights in Nations and in Religions*, ed. Leonard Swidler,
       167-174. Philadelphia and New York: Ecumenical Press and
       Hippocrene Books, 1986.

       See the annotation at entry 150.

320   Berinson, Zvi. "Freedom of Religion and Conscience in the State of
       Israel." *Israel Yearbook on Human Rights* 3 (1973): 223-232.

       The author studies how Israel's self-understanding as a Jewish state
       threatens its citizens freedom of conscience. He notes that Israel's
       commitment to freedom of conscience stands on shaky legal grounds.
       The law, while formally allowing conversion, makes this difficult by
       demanding assent from the head of the authorized body of the
       religious group being joined.

321   Bick, Etta, ed. "Sheat Hadechak." In her *Judaic Sources of Human Rights*,
       16-44. Tel Aviv: Israel-Diaspora Institute, 1987.

       See the annotation at entry 169.

322 Bracha, Baruch. *Equality Before the Law*. Jerusalem: The Association for Civil Rights in Israel, 1989. Hebrew.

This book looks at the situation of the law in Israel and its treatment of different groups in the population. Not only its application to the Jewish State, but its sensitivity to the problem of religion in such a state makes it relevant to the study of Judaism and human rights.

323 Bracha, Baruch. "Personal Status of Persons Belonging to No Recognized Religious Community." *Israel Yearbook on Human Rights* 5 (1975): 88-119.

See the annotation at entry 182.

324 Carmon, Arye, Prologue. In *Judaic Sources of Human Rights*, ed. Etta Bick, vii-viii. Tel Aviv: Israel-Diaspora Institute, 1987.

See the annotation at entry 193.

325 Cohn, Haim H. "Israeli Law and the Rights of the Individual." *Congress Monthly* 45, 3 (1978): 14-17, 20-21.

Cohn (spelled here Cohen) reviews Israeli procedure in terms of its respect for human rights. He surveys rights of the accused and of the prosecution, rights to petition, privacy, and free speech. He notes some problems in Israel's approach to censorship (the music of Wagner and Richard Strauss is proscribed in what Cohn calls a manner reminiscent of Nazi thinking). His most severe criticism is against the restrictions on freedom of religion made for the sake of appeasing Orthodox Jewish leaders. The discussion and Cohn's response focus on this final issue.

326 Dinstein, Yoram. "Discrimination and International Human Rights." *Israel Yearbook on Human Rights* 15 (1985): 11-17.

The author claims that not every type of discrimination is incompatible with a concern for human rights. Thus the right to freedom of religion (i.e. to public worship) may be infringed without religious discrimination when public safety is threatened or that public religious ceremonies may not always constitute an infringement on freedom of religion. Jewish law, in this regard, only appears to contradict the right of freedom of conscience.

327   Gavison, Ruth. *Civil Rights and Democracy*. Jerusalem: The Association
       for Civil Rights in Israel, 1988. Hebrew.

   Gavison examines the relationship between the ideals and practice of
   democracy and the maintenance of civil rights for all citizens with
   particular reference to the situation in the State of Israel.

328   Gavison, Ruth. "The Controversy Over Israel's Bill of Rights." *Israel
       Yearbook on Human Rights* 15 (1985): 113-154.

   Gavison argues that the Israeli Parliament, the Kenesset, does indeed
   enact basic laws.   She claims that changing the name of the
   Constituent Assembly to the Kenesset meant deemphasizing need to
   create a constitution.   She agrees that Israel's eight basic laws would
   be difficult to mold into a constitution and suggests instead the
   composing of a Bill of Rights in one single, entrenched, supreme
   enactment that highlights concisely the values and rights to which the
   State is committed.   She notes the arguments against enacting such
   a Bill of Rights, but concludes that the temptations to violate rights
   in Israel's dangerous political situation may require just such a
   guarantee.

329   Gavison, Ruth. "Introduction." In her *Civil Rights in Israel*, 9-46.
       Jerusalem: The Association for Civil Rights in Israel, 1982. Hebrew.

   Gavison notes Cohn's devotion to the many-sided issue of civil rights
   throughout his career. She distinguishes between legal, traditional,
   ideal, and natural rights.   She also mentions the infractions to
   freedom of religion caused by Israel's laws which may infringe on
   the rights of both Jews who are non-religious and of non-Jews. This
   introduction does more than present biographical information; it also
   provides a theoretical foundation for discussion issues of conscience
   and law as part of universal human rights.

330   Gendler, Everett E. "War and the Jewish Tradition." In *Contemporary
       Jewish Ethics*, ed. Menahem M. Kellner, 189-210.   David M. L.
       Olivestone, series ed., Sanhedrin Jewish Studies. New York:
       Sanhedrin, 1978.

   Gendler recognizes that the Jewish tradition cannot be called pacifist
   but he emphasizes the various duties that the state and individual
   must perform that protect certain rights such as those to life,
   freedom of conscience, and self-defense. The article is useful in its
   ability to intertwine references to classical texts with a passionate
   appeal for peace and the protection of human rights.

331   Landman, Leo. "Law and Conscience: The Jewish View." *Judaism* 18
      (1969): 17-29.

      See the annotation at entry 107.

332   Rackman, Emanuel. "Talmudic Insights on Human Rights." *Judaism* 1
      (1952): 158-162.

      See the annotation at entry 121.

333   Rubinstein, Amnon. "The Struggle Over a Bill of Rights for Israel." In
      Constitutionalism: The Israeli and American Experiences, ed. Daniel
      J. Elazar, 139-142. Lanham, MD: University Press of America,
      1990.

      See the annotation at entry 286.

334   Schneider, Hagi. *Freedom of Religion in Israel*.   Jerusalem: The
      Association for Civil Rights in Israel, 1990. Hebrew.

      This workbook prepared by Hagi Schneider looks at the various
      religious communities in Israel, including the different streams of
      Jewish religion. In this way he surveys the Jewish approaches to
      freedom of conscience. He shows the problems for the preservation
      of religious rights arising from the creation of a self-avowed 'Jewish
      State.'

335   Weiler, Gershon. "On Freedom of Religion and Worship." In *Human
      Rights in Israel: Articles in Memory of Judge Haman Shelah*, ed.
      Ann Swersky, 22-35. Tel Aviv: Edanim and Yediot Aharonot, 1988.
      Hebrew.

      See the annotation at entry 140.

336   Wyschogrod, Michael. "Judaism and Conscience." In *Standing Before God:
      Studies on Prayer in Scriptures and in Tradition with Essays In
      Honor of John M. Oesterreicher*, eds. Asher Finkel and Lawrence
      Frizzell, 313-328. New York: Ktav, 1981

      See the annotation at entry 143.

337   Zeltner, Zeev. "Human Rights Considered as Religious Rights." *Tel Aviv
      University Law Review (Iyyunei Mishpat)* 3, 1 (1978): 5-13.

      See the annotation at entry 145.

THE RIGHT OF DISSENT

338   Braude, Samuel G. "Civil Disobedience and the Jewish Tradition." In *Judaism and Ethics*, ed. Daniel Jeremy Silver, 229-239. New York: Ktav, 1970.

See the annotation at entry 183.

339   Cohn, Haim H. "The Right and Duty of Resistance." *Revue des Droits de l'Homme. Human Rights Journal* 1, 4 (1968): 491-516.

Cohn discusses the right and moral imperative to dissent from and resist unjust governments and unjust orders.

340   Gordis, Robert. "The Right of Dissent and Intellectual Liberty." In *Judaism and Human Rights*, ed. Milton R. Konvitz, 190-211. New York: W. W. Norton, 1972.

See the annotation at entry 081.

341   Greenberg, Moshe. "Rabbinic Reflections on Defying Illegal Orders: Amasa, Abner, and Joab." In *Contemporary Jewish Ethics*, ed. Menahem M. Kellner, 211-220.   David M. L. Olivestone, series ed., Sanhedrin Jewish Studies. New York: Sanhedrin, 1978.

See the annotation at entry 082.

342   Israel, Rachel. "Judaisme et Dissidence." In *Judaisme et Droits de l'Homme*, ed. Emmanuel Hirsch, 189-198. Paris: Librairie des Libertés, 1984. French.

See the annotation at entry 095.

343   Kimmelman, Reuven. "The Rabbinic Ethics of Protest." *Judaism* 19 (1970): 38-58.

See the annotation at entry 101.

344   Lamm, Maurice. "After the War - Another Look at Pacifism and Selective Conscientious Objection (SCO)." In *Contemporary Jewish Ethics*, ed. Menahem M. Kellner, 221-238.   David M. L. Olivestone, series ed., Sanhedrin Jewish Studies. New York: Sanhedrin, 1978.

Lamm goes beyond citing Jewish sources to answer the question of whether Jews support the right to political dissent and the right for peace rather than war. He considers the ideal of pacifism itself and contends that it represents a utopian and unrealistic model. He rejects it on the grounds of its flawed vision rather than because of traditional Jewish texts. He also rejects an unlimited right to dissent on the grounds that such a right impairs the ability of society to function. The members of a group must relinquish some personal rights for the sake of the greater good of all.

345   Landman, Leo. "Law and Conscience: The Jewish View." *Judaism* 18 (1969): 17-29.

See the annotation at entry 107.

346   Rackman, Emanuel. "Talmudic Insights on Human Rights." *Judaism* 1 (1952): 158-162.

See the annotation at entry 121.

347   Sheleff, Leon. "Conscientious Dissent from the Law." In *Civil Rights in Israel*, ed. Ruth Gavison, 117-151. Jerusalem: The Association for Civil Rights in Israel, 1982. Hebrew.

The author looks at some instances of civil disobedience, especially of conscientious objection during wartime, with reference to general political and philosophical studies as well as particular cases in Israel.

THE RIGHT TO EQUALITY

348   Altmann, Alexander. "Moses Mendelssohn as the Archetypal German Jew." In *The Jewish Response to German Culture From the Enlightenment to the Second World War*, eds. Jehuda Reinharz and Walter Schatzberg, 17-31. Hanover, NH: University Press of New England, 1985.

See the annotation at entry 152.

349   Baron, Salo Wittmayer. *The Russian Jew Under Tsars and Soviets*. New York: Macmillan, 1976.

See the annotation at entry 161.

350   Belkin, Samuel. "The Equality of Man." In his *In His Image: The Jewish Philosophy of Man as Expressed in Rabbinic Tradition*, 60-78. Westport, CT: Greenwood, 1979.

    See the annotation at entry 050.

351   Ben-Gal, Teli. *The Right to Equality*. Jerusalem: The Association for Civil Rights in Israel, 1990. Hebrew.

    See the annotation at entry 166.

352   Ben-Gal, Teli and Zoref, Zivka, eds. *Civil Rights in Israel*. Jerusalem: The Association for Civil Rights in Israel, 1988. Hebrew.

    See the annotation at entry 167.

353   Bieber, Hans-Joachim. "Anti-Semitism as a Reflection of Social, Economic and Political Tension in Germany: 1880-1933." In *Jews and Germans From 1860-1933: The Problematic Symbiosis*, ed. David Bronsen, 33-77. Heidelberg: Carl Winter, 1979.

    Modernization and Emancipation began together in Germany and German Jews espoused both. Antisemitism as a political policy often expressed social and political concerns and many members of the political and economic elite were not antisemites in their private lives. He denies that assimilation caused the Nazi era and asks instead how assimilation can lead to co-existence and symbiosis rather than destructiveness.

354   Borowitz, Eugene B. "Social Justice, the Liberal Jewish Case." In his *Exploring Jewish Ethics: Papers on Covenant Responsibility*, 295-307. Detroit, MI: Wayne State University Press, 1990.

    See the annotation at entry 060.

355   Bracha, Baruch. *Equality Before the Law*. Jerusalem: The Association for Civil Rights in Israel, 1989. Hebrew.

    See the annotation at entry 322.

356   Bronsen, David. "Foreword." In *Jews and Germans From 1860-1933: The Problematic Symbiosis*, ed. David Bronsen, 1-8. Heidelberg: Carl Winter, 1979.

    See the annotation at entry 186.

357   Cohn, Haim H. "Rights of Equality." In his *Human Rights in Jewish Law*, 149-186. New York: Ktav, 1984.

Cohn focuses on the teachings of Judaism as applied to various social minorities such as those occasioned by gender, race, religion, birth, property, or citizenship. He suggests that Jewish law engenders tolerance and protection of minorities.

358   Finkelstein, Louis. "The Hebrew Doctrine of Equality." *Menorah Journal* 24 (1936): 16-29.

See the annotation at entry 074.

359   Finkelstein, Louis. "Human Equality in the Jewish Tradition." *Conservative Judaism* 10, 1 (1955): 1-27.

See the annotation at entry 075.

360   Gilman, Sander. "Karl Marx and the Secret Language of Jews." *Modern Judaism* 4, 3 (1984): 275-294.

See the annotation at entry 216.

361   Guttmann, Alexander. "The Role of Equity in the History of the Halakhah." In *Julius Mark Jubilee Volume*, eds. Ronald Sobel and Sidney Wallach, 71-92. New York: Ktav, 1975.

See the annotation at entry 083.

362   Herzog, Yitzhak Isaac HaLevi. "Minority Rights According to Halacha." *Techumin: Torah, Society, and State: Compendium of Halakha* 2 (1981): 169-79.

Herzog emphasizes that Jewish tradition ensures equality of treatment as a basic right for both Jew and non-Jew within any society. He calls upon the State of Israel to exemplify this traditional value. He therefore roots the principles of equality before the law and fair treatment to minorities in Jewish tradition and demands the application of those principles in the modern Jewish state.

363   Heschel, Abraham Joshua. "A Declaration of Conscience." In his *The Insecurity of Freedom: Essays on Human Existence*, 274-284. New York: Schocken, 1972.

See the annotation at entry 087.

364   Heschel, Abraham Joshua. "Religion and Race." In his *The Insecurity of Freedom: Essays on Human Existence*, 85-100. New York: Schocken, 1972.

See the annotation at entry 091.

365   Heschel, Abraham Joshua. "Sacred Image of Man." In his *The Insecurity of Freedom: Essays on Human Existence*, 150-167. New York: Schocken, 1972.

See the annotation at entry 093.

366   Heschel, Abraham Joshua. "The White Man on Trial." In his *The Insecurity of Freedom: Essays on Human Existence*, 101-111. New York: Schocken, 1972.

See the annotation at entry 094.

367   Israel, Rachel. "Judaisme et Dissidence." In *Judaisme et Droits de l'Homme*, ed. Emmanuel Hirsch, 189-198. Paris: Librairie des Libertés, 1984. French.

See the annotation at entry 095.

368   Jakobovits, Immanuel. "Anti-Semitism: After the Holocaust, After the State of Israel." In *Anti-Semitism and Human Rights*, ed. Serge Liberman, 1-6, 34-35. North Melbourne, Vic.: Australian Institute of Jewish Affairs, 1985.

The author contends that the vocabulary of inhumanity uses words drawn from Jewish experience like racism, genocide, holocaust, pogroms, and ghetto. He suggests that the Jewish struggle for equal rights has been the prototype for the human rights movements of the contemporary world. Thus Judaism provides the basic example of a religion that grants all human beings an inherent right to equal treatment. Given this philosophy, however, the author condemns slogans such as "Never Again" as debilitating substitutes for positive Jewish values. In response to questioning, Jakobovits, argues that Jews have been deeply concerned with all struggles for human rights.

369   Katz, Nathan. "Jewish Perspectives on Equality." *Ethnic Studies Report* IV, 1 (January 1986): 64-70.

See the annotation at entry 099.

370   Low, Alfred D. *Jews in the Eyes of the Germans: From the Enlightenment to Imperial Germany*. Philadelphia: Institute for the Study of Human Issues, 1979.

See the annotation at entry 259.

371   Meron, Theodor. *Human Rights Law-Making in the United Nations: A Critique of Instruments and Process*. Oxford: Clarendon Press, 1986.

Meron notes several issues concerning Judaism in this wide-ranging and detailed review of the United Nations conventions on human rights. He notes, for example, that while not explicitly mentioned, antisemitism falls under and provided the motivation for the convention against racial discrimination. He also notes the conflict that can arise from cultural differences in applying the conventions, since Jewish law seems to imply an unequal distribution of rights between men and women, and he discusses the ramifications of this conflict.

372   Novak, David. "Lex Talionis: A Maimonidean Perspective on Scripture, Tradition and Reason." *S'vara: A Journal of Philosophy and Judaism* 1, 2 (1991): 61-64.

Novak investigates the idea of human equality and its application in criminal law. He emphasizes the inherent value Judaism places on the individual's life since it is not evaluated in terms of its value for a greater whole.

373   Plaskow, Judith. *Standing Again At Sinai: Judaism From a Feminist Perspective*. San Francisco: Harper and Row, 1990.

This creative theological work repeatedly returns to the theme of equality. Not merely are Jewish women denied equal rights in the Jewish religious system. That system itself needs revision. As traditionally imagined it projects an inequitable view of reality that expresses a purely male point of view. Equality under the old system cannot satisfy the Jewish woman who must, instead, seek a radical altering of the Jewish religious program. Plaskow's call for such radical behavior advances an important vision of human rights broadly conceived.

374   Polish, Daniel F. "Judaism and Human Rights." In *Human Rights in Religious Traditions*, ed. Arlene Swidler, 40-50. New York: Pilgrim, 1982.

See the annotation at entry 117.

375   Pulzer, Peter. "Jewish Participation in Wilhelmine Politics." In *Jews and Germans From 1860-1933: The Problematic Symbiosis*, ed. David Bronsen, 78-99. Heidelberg: Carl Winter, 1979.

See the annotation at entry 273.

376   Rabinowitz, Louis. "The Rights of the Individual (a response to Aharon Lichtenstein)." *Congress Monthly* 45, 3 (1978): 8-9.

See the annotation at entry 118.

377   Rackman, Emanuel. "A God Centered Humanism." In his *One Man's Judaism*, 149-171. New York: Philosophical Library, 1971.

See the annotation at entry 119.

378   Rackman, Emanuel. "Judaism and Equality." In his *One Man's Judaism*, 120-145. New York: Philosophical Library, 1971.

See the annotation at entry 120.

379   Rotenstreich, Nathan. "For and Against Emancipation: The Bruno Bauer Controversy." *The Leo Baeck Institute Yearbook* 4 (1959): 3-36.

See the annotation at entry 279.

380   Rotenstreich, Nathan. *Jew and German Philosophy: The Polemics of Emancipation*. New York: Schocken, 1984.

See the annotation at entry 280.

381   Rotenstreich, Nathan. "Of Equality." In his *Order and Might*, 185-207. Albany, NY: State University of New York Press, 1988.

Rotenstreich suggests that the variety of theories of equality represent a single search for that which is typically human. Some theories begin with empirical diversity and others with a general theory of human nature. The idea of equality serves to regulate demands people make on society in the name of a transcendent value. It acts as an interpretation of the idea of justice rather than as an exclusive norm. The idea of equality provides the starting point for political agitation. The goal of equality, taken as an end in itself, shapes the role and function of politics which seeks to attain that end.

382   Samuels, Shimon. "Anti-Semitism: The Abiding Prejudice." In *Anti-Semitism and Human Rights*, ed. Serge Liberman, 15-18, 35-36. North Melbourne, Vic.: Australian Institute of Jewish Affairs, 1985.

Samuels argues that the strategy of Arab terrorism is to isolate the Jewish citizen as a creature apart and thus worthy of fewer rights than other human beings. He claims that just as the existence of marriage creates the possibility of divorce so the existence of democracy and pluralism testifies to the possibilities of prejudice and antisemitism. He argues for the existence of a trans-national, trans-ideological antisemitism that undermines any ideal of human rights with an abiding prejudice. In response to questioning he noted the efforts that the Anti-Defamation League of B'nai B'rith, a Jewish group, makes on behalf of all peoples.

383 Walzer, Michael. *Spheres of Justice: A Defense of Pluralism and Equality.* New York: Basic Books, 1983.

See the annotation at entry 139.

384 Weltsch, Robert. "Introduction." *Leo Baeck Institute Yearbook* 4 (1959): ix-xxvi.

Weltsch's introduction to this volume shows how Jews adjusted their policy throughout the nineteenth century to affirm their claim to equal rights in the German state. As visions of the national state fluctuated, so various idéologies supporting the Jewish claim to rights also varied. Thus he argues that in their struggle for full citizenship the Jews had to adapt their reasoning to the arguments of their adversaries.

FREEDOM OF EXPRESSION

385 Barak, Aaron. "Judicial Perspectives: The View from Israel." In *The Constitutional Bases of Political and Social Change in the United States*, ed. Shlomo Slonim, 287-294. Westport, CT: Praeger, 1990.

Barak notes several differences between Israel and the United States on constitutional issues. He suggests that the principles of freedom of expression, of movement, of association, and of occupation are a source of individual rights according to Israel's common law, and therefore, Israel does not need a constitution. He considers the difference between such common law consensus and the case of a constitutional guarantee overly exaggerated.

386 Cantor, Norman L. "On Clear and Present Danger, Clear Probability, and Free Speech Standards in Israel." *Israel Yearbook on Human Rights* 16 (1986): 260-290.
Cantor notes that the Israeli legal system was influenced by American free speech jurisprudence as it existed in 1953. Nevertheless, he notes and approves of the censorship carried out in

the occupied territories. He notes that Israeli law is wary of granting too much freedom because of the experience of the Nazi rise to power in which democratic tools were utilized to destroy a democratic regime.

387   Carmilly-Weinberger, Moshe. *Book and Sword: Freedom of Expression and Thought Among the Jewish People.* New York: Shulsinger Brothers, 1966. Hebrew.

See the annotation at entry 064.

388   Chafets, Zeev. "Press and Government in Israel." *Israel Yearbook on Human Rights* 14 (1984): 134-17.

Chafets describes Israel's military censorship of the press despite a declared commitment to freedom of the press. He sees it as a compromise between Israel's security needs and its desire for a democracy. He recounts events illustrating the delicate balance Israel maintains in this regard.

389   Cohn, Haim H. "Israeli Law and the Rights of the Individual." *Congress Monthly* 45, 3 (1978): 14-17, 20-21.

See the annotation at entry 325.

390   Cohn, Haim H. "La Liberté de Pensée et de Parole en Droit Juif." In *Judaisme et Droits de l'Homme*, ed. Emmanuel Hirsch, 54-83. Idéologies et Droits de l'Homme   B.01. Paris: Librairie des Libertés, 1984. French.

See the annotation at entry 070.

391   Kushner, Harold S. "A Jewish View of Verbal and Visual Obscenity." *Proceedings of the Rabbinical Assembly* 40 (1978): 102-107.

See the annotation at entry 104.

392 Levinas, Emmanuel. "Liberté de Parole." In his *Difficile Liberté: Essais sur le Judaisme*, 265-268. Presences Du Judaisme. Paris: Albin Michel, 1963. French.

Levinas notes that the flagrant manufacturing of "fact" by Russian leaders parallels the development of language in the West. Freedom of speech means nothing when language has no inherent meaning. In such a situation a prophetic word alone can penetrate the falsity of language. See the translation by Sean Hand in *Difficult Freedom: Essays on Judaism*. Baltimore: Johns Hopkins University Press, 1990, 205-207.

393 Urian, Meir. "Civil Liberty and Freedom of Expression." In his *In the Circle of Hassidism and in the Paths of Our Time*, 250-254. Jerusalem: Rubin Mass, 1977. Hebrew.

See the annotation at entry 137.

394 Weiler, Gershon. "Religion and Human Rights in Israel." *Index on Censorship* 5 (October 1983): 7-9.

Weiler notes that two factors circumscribe the scope of human rights in Israel: it is a country of the Eastern Mediterranean and it is Jewish. He traces the historical problems which Israel inherited and the uneasy compromise between political Zionism and Jewish religion. This compromise exacerbates the problem of ensuring citizenship rights based on political rather than religious considerations. He suggests that the conscience of one part of the Israeli society takes precedence over that of others. He considers various examples of the problem of human rights: the Law of Return, marriage and divorce laws, and the complexity of rule over the non-Jewish Arab population. This has been reprinted as *Religion and Human Rights in Israel*, London: Writers and Scholars International, 1983.

THE RIGHT TO RAISE A FAMILY

395 Ahroni, Reuben. "The Levirate and Human Rights." *Jewish Law and Current Legal Problems*, ed. Nahum Rakover, 67-76. Library of Jewish Law. Jerusalem: Jewish Legal Heritage Society, 1984.

See the annotation at entry 042.

396   Bokser, Ben Zion. "Democratic Aspirations in Talmudic Judaism." In *Judaism and Human Rights*, ed. Milton R. Konvitz, 145-155. New York: W. W. Norton, 1972.

See the annotation at entry 058.

397   Goitein, S. D. "Human Rights in Jewish Thought and Life in the Middle Ages." In *Essays on Human Rights: Contemporary Issues and Jewish Perspectives*, eds. David Sidorsky, *et al.*, 247-264. Philadelphia: Jewish Publication Society, 1979.

See the annotation at entry 079.

398   Rackman, Emanuel. "Judaism and Equality." In his *One Man's Judaism*, 120-145. New York: Philosophical Library, 1971.

See the annotation at entry 120.

399   Roth, Sol. "Human Rights." In his *Halakhah and Politics: The Jewish Idea of the State*, 117-128.   Norman Lamm, series ed., The Library of Jewish Law and Ethics 14. Hoboken, NJ: Ktav, 1988.

See the annotation at entry 283.

400   Shelach, Chaman P. "Freedom of Conscience and Freedom of Heart." In *Civil Rights in Israel*, ed. Ruth Gavison, 85-115. Jerusalem: The Association for Civil Rights in Israel, 1982. Hebrew.

Shelah seeks a balance between the freedom necessary for individuals seeking free practice of their religion and freedom of conscience for all citizens, whether religious or secular.   As examples he examines modern judicial decisions in Israel, the question of a common law marriage, and of Karaite marriages. He concludes that the rule of Jewish law abridges some human rights.

401   Weiler, Gershon. "Religion and Human Rights in Israel." *Index on Censorship* 5 (October 1983): 7-9.

See the annotation at entry 394.

402   Zohar, Noam. "Artificial Insemination and Surrogate Motherhood." *S'vara: A Journal of Philosophy and Judaism* 1, 2 (1991): 13-19.

Zohar argues both for a right to found a family and limitations to that right. He claims that the halakhah seeks to create an egalitarian control over reproduction rights, even though the restriction of autonomy imposed on each partner may be asymmetrical.

THE RIGHT TO FREEDOM

403   Belkin, Samuel. "The Sacredness of Human Life." In his *In His Image: The Jewish Philosophy of Man as Expressed in Rabbinic Tradition*, 97-116. Westport, CT: Greenwood, 1979.

See the annotation at entry 053.

404   Carmi, Amnon. "Freedom and Human Rights." In his *On Law and Medicine*, 15-27. Haifa: Tamar, 1987.

See the annotation at entry 191.

405   Rotenstreich, Nathan. "Of Freedom." In his *Order and Might*.   Albany, NY: State University of New York Press, 1988.

Using the Nazi persecution of Jews as a primary case study, Rotenstreich argues that rights are a means of defining the freedom possible within the realm of political systems.

406   Warhaftig, Itamar. "The Ethics of Using Prisoners for Experimentation." *Techumin: Torah, Society, and State: Compendium of Halakha* 1 (1980): 530-536.

Warhaftig argues on the basis of Jewish respect for life that although prisoners are coerced bodily, he suggests, their free will should not be constrained as such experimentation would do.

THE RIGHT TO HEALTH

407   Bardfelt, Philip A. "Jewish Medical Ethics." *Reconstructionist* 42, 6 (1976): 7-11.

See the annotation at entry 046.

408   Bulka, Reuven. "The Role of the Individual in Jewish Law." *Tradition* 13/14 (1973): 124-136.

See the annotation at entry 187.

409   Carmi, Amnon. "Freedom and Human Rights." In his *On Law and Medicine*, 15-27. Haifa: Tamar, 1987.

See the annotation at entry 191.

410   Carmi, Amnon. "No Treatment - No Compensation." In his *Law and Medicine*, 294-308. Haifa: Tamar, 1987.

The study surveys several cases in which an injured worker demanded continued compensation for an injury despite a refusal to have the injury medically treated. Carmi begins by noting that all human beings have a right to self-determination about the disposition of their own bodies. He claims, however, that this right should be limited by considerations of reasonableness and safety.

411   Heschel, Abraham Joshua. "The Patient as Person." In his *The Insecurity of Freedom: Essays on Human Existence*, 24-38. New York: Schocken, 1972.

See the annotation at entry 090.

412   Rackman, Emanuel. "Medical-Legal Problems." In his *One Man's Judaism*, 107-119. New York: Philosophical Library, 1971.

Rackman surveys a patient's right to know the truth of a diagnosis and also the patient's right to privacy. He maintains that Judaism emphasizes the duty aspect of the correlative terms of rights and duties. He investigates the extent to which the principle of self-defense may be invoked in favor of contraception and sterilization.

413   Sherwin, Byron L. "Health, Healing and Tradition." In his *In Partnership with God: Contemporary Jewish Law and Ethics*, 66-84. Syracuse: Syracuse University Press, 1990

See the annotation at entry 128.

THE RIGHTS OF LABOR

414   Atlas, Samuel. "Rights of Private Property and Private Profit." *Central Conference of American Rabbis Yearbook* 54 (1944): 212-256.

See the annotation at entry 155.

415   Ben-Israel, Ruth. "Is the Right to Strike a Collective Human Right?" *Israel Yearbook on Human Rights* 11 (1981): 195-216.

This study of the right to strike has particular relevance here since the author focuses on that right as practiced in the modern state of Israel and as a reflection of the values of a Jewish state.

416   Bokser, Ben Zion. "Democratic Aspirations in Talmudic Judaism." In
        Judaism and Human Rights, ed. Milton R. Konvitz, 145-155. New
        York: W. W. Norton, 1972.

        See the annotation at entry 058.

417   Carmi, Amnon. "No Treatment - No Compensation." In his *Law and
        Medicine*, 294-308. Haifa: Tamar, 1987.

        See the annotation at entry 410.

418   Kaplan, Mordecai M. *The Meaning of God in Jewish Religion*. New York:
        Reconstructionist, 1962.

        See the annotation at entry 098.

419   Levine, Aaron. *Economics and Jewish Law*. Norman Lamm, series ed.,
        The Library of Jewish Law and Ethics 13. Hoboken, NJ and New
        York: Ktav and Yeshivah University Press, 1987.

        The author argues that Jewish law intervenes in the market place to
        impose moral prescriptions that force on market participants a higher
        ethical standard than the profit motive. He includes "the right to
        know" as a commercial limitation on profiteering. He suggests
        certain rights of the seller and of prospective buyers. Part of his
        investigation focuses on social welfare and the actualization of a
        social welfare philosophy which he bases on the human principle of
        loving the other as oneself. He also studies labor relations and the
        rights of both workers and employers.

420   Rackman, Emanuel. "Talmudic Insights on Human Rights." *Judaism* 1
        (1952): 158-162.

        See the annotation at entry 121.

421   Walzer, Michael. "Free Time." In his *Spheres of Justice: A Defense of
        Pluralism and Equality*, 184-196. New York: Basic Books, 1983

        See the annotation at entry 138.

THE RIGHT TO LEGAL EQUITY

422   Agus, Irving A. "The Rights and Immunities of the Minority." *Jewish
        Quarterly Review*, n.s. 45 (1954-55): 120-129.

        See the annotation at entry 149.

423   Barak, Aaron. "Judicial Perspectives: The View from Israel." In *The Constitutional Bases of Political and Social Change in the United States*, ed. Shlomo Slonim, 287-294. Westport, CT: Praeger, 1990.

See the annotation at entry 385.

424   Belkin, Samuel. "The Equality of Man." In his *In His Image: The Jewish Philosophy of Man as Expressed in Rabbinic Tradition*, 60-78. Westport, CT: Greenwood, 1979.

See the annotation at entry 050.

425   Belkin, Samuel. "Man and His Trustworthiness." In his *In His Image: The Jewish Philosophy of Man as Expressed in Rabbinic Tradition*, 79-96. Westport, CT: Greenwood, 1979.

See the annotation at entry 052.

426   Bracha, Baruch. *Equality Before the Law*. Jerusalem: The Association for Civil Rights in Israel, 1989. Hebrew.

See the annotation at entry 322.

427   Bracha, Baruch. "Personal Status of Persons Belonging to No Recognized Religious Community." *Israel Yearbook on Human Rights* 5 (1975): 88-119.

See the annotation at entry 182.

428   Byrd, B. Sharon. "Justice and Talionis." *S'vara: A Journal of Philosophy and Judaism* 1, 2 (1991): 65-68.

See the annotation at entry 188.

429   Calef, Michel. "Un Regard Juif sur l'Ambiguite des Droits de l'Homme." In *Judaisme et Droits de l'Homme*, ed. Emmanuel Hirsch, 133-160. Idéologies et Droits de l'Homme   B.01. Paris: Librairie des Libertés, 1984. French.

See the annotation at entry 189.

430   Carmon, Arye, Prologue. In *Judaic Sources of Human Rights*, ed. Etta Bick, vii-viii. Tel Aviv: Israel-Diaspora Institute, 1987.

See the annotation at entry 193.

431   Cohn, Haim H. "Israeli Law and the Rights of the Individual." *Congress Monthly* 45, 3 (1978): 14-17, 20-21.

See the annotation at entry 325.

432   Cohn, Haim H. "Rights of Justice." In his *Human Rights in Jewish Law*, 187-216. New York: Ktav, 1984.

Cohn enumerates various procedural directives in Jewish law and shows how they protect such rights as self-defense, the right of non-self-incrimination, and the right to a fair, speedy, and just trial.

433   Cohn, Haim H. "Torture and Cruel Punishments." In his *Human Rights in Jewish Law*, 217-224. New York: Ktav, 1984.

Cohn doubts the justice of several forms of punishment, including the death penalty and argues for mitigating punishment through a consideration of human rights.

434   Daube, David. "The Rabbis and Philo on Human Rights." In *Human Rights in Essays on Human Rights: Contemporary Issues and Jewish Perspectives*, ed. David Sidorsky, *et al.*, 234-246. Philadelphia: Jewish Publication Society, 1979.

See the annotation at entry 071.

435   Gavison, Ruth. "The Controversy Over Israel's Bill of Rights." *Israel Yearbook on Human Rights* 15 (1985): 113-154.

See the annotation at entry 328.

436   Gavison, Ruth. "Introduction." In her *Civil Rights in Israel*, 9-46. Jerusalem: The Association for Civil Rights in Israel, 1982. Hebrew.

See the annotation at entry 329.

437   Gershuni, Jehudah. "Minority Rights in the State of Israel in the Light of Halacha." *Techumin: Torah, Society, and State: Compendium of Halakha* 2 (1981): 180-192.

Gershuni struggles to determine the rights of non-Jews in the State of Israel on the basis of traditional Jewish law. He suggests, however, that many aspects of Jewish law can no longer be practiced. He claims that the need for peace outweighs the precedent of Jewish law which once placed disabilities on minorities in the land of Israel.

438   Goodman, Lenn Evan. *On Justice: An Essay in Jewish Philosophy*. New Haven: Yale University Press, 1991.

See the annotation at entry 220.

439   Kirschenbaum, Aaron. "Jewish Law and the Abuse of Rights." *Tel Aviv University Studies in Law* 5 (1980/1982): 98-114.

See the annotation at entry 242.

440   Konvitz, Milton R. "Torah and Constitution : An American Bicentennial Lecture." *Proceedings of the Rabbinical Assembly* 38 (1976): 54-67.

See the annotation at entry 103.

441   Lamm, Norman. "The Fifth Amendment and its Equivalent in the Halakha." *Judaism* 5 (1956): 53-59.

Lamm claims that the Halakha has a more powerful basis for its rejection of self-incrimination than American law. The latter forbids self-incrimination to limit the possibility of torturing a confession. Judaism invalidates all confessions because human beings should not consider themselves evil. In this way the halakha recognizes but seeks to overcome what Freud called each person's 'death-wish.'

442   Landau, Lazare. "Judaisme et Droits de l'Homme." In *Judaisme et Droits de l'Homme*, ed. Emmanuel Hirsch, 59-63. Idéologies et Droits de l'Homme B.01. Paris: Librairie des Libertés, 1984. French.

See the annotation at entry 105.

443   Landau, Moshe. "The Limits of Constitutions and Judicial Review." In *Constitutionalism: The Israeli and American Experiences*, ed. Daniel J. Elazar, 197-205. Lanham, MD: University Press of America, 1990.

See the annotation at entry 106.

444   Levin, Stanley. "Due Process in Rabbinical and Israeli Law: Abuse and Subversion." In *Jewish Law and Current Legal Problems*, ed. Nahum Rakover, 191-194. Library of Jewish Law Jerusalem: Jewish Legal Heritage Society, 1984.

See the annotation at entry 108.

445   Malamud-Goti, Jaime. "Punishment and Human Dignity." *S'vara: A Journal of Philosophy and Judaism* 1, 2 (1991): 69-71.

Malamud-Goti argues that retributive justice is actually utilitarian and has a goal beyond making the criminal suffer. Indeed, he thinks that punishing official lawlessness actually fosters an affirmation of personal rights. Because such punishment acknowledges the victim's inherent worth, it encourages the victim to participate as a full member in the rights-based society. He claims that punishment in dictatorial regimes, for example in the trials by Argentine's government, fails to achieve the utilitarian goals that retributive punishment in Jewish law achieves.

446   Meislin, B. J. "Refusal to Testify as a Protected First Amendment Religious Right." *Jewish Law Annual* 1 (1978): 219-221.

See the annotation at entry 113.

447   Novak, David. "Lex Talionis: A Maimonidean Perspective on Scripture, Tradition and Reason." *S'vara: A Journal of Philosophy and Judaism* 1, 2 (1991): 61-64.

See the annotation at entry 372.

448   Polish, Daniel F. "Judaism and Human Rights." In *Human Rights in Religious Traditions*, ed. Arlene Swidler, 40-50. New York: Pilgrim, 1982.

See the annotation at entry 117.

449   Rackman, Emanuel. "Talmudic Insights on Human Rights." *Judaism* 1 (1952): 158-162.

See the annotation at entry 121.

450   Rotenstreich, Nathan. "Of Justice." In his *Order and Might*, 107-134. Albany, NY: State University of New York Press, 1988.

Rotenstreich claims that justice consists of balancing rights and duties. He argues that the state as an impersonal force that transcends special interests plays a significant role in realizing such a balance of rights and duties. He notes that Jews during the period of Emancipation based their claim to rights on the principle of justice, that is on the idea of equally treatment under the law.

451   Roth, Sol. "Human Rights." In his *Halakhah and Politics: The Jewish Idea of the State*, 117-128. Norman Lamm, series ed., The Library of Jewish Law and Ethics 14. Hoboken, NJ: Ktav, 1988.

See the annotation at entry 283.

452   Rubinstein, Amnon. "The Struggle Over a Bill of Rights for Israel." In *Constitutionalism: The Israeli and American Experiences*, ed. Daniel J. Elazar, 139-142. Lanham, MD: University Press of America, 1990.

See the annotation at entry 286.

453   Shilo, S. "Kofin Al Midat S'dom: Jewish Law's Concept of Abuse of Rights." *Tel Aviv University Law Review (Iyyunei Mishpat)* 15 (1980/82): 49-114.

See the annotation at entry 292.

454   Slonim, Shlomo. "Preface." In *The Constitutional Bases of Political and Social Change in the United States*, ed. Shlomo Slonim, ix-xiii. Westport, CT: Praeger, 1990.

The preface notes both how American Jews have enjoyed equality and freedom in the United States and how Israel, as a nation, has benefitted from this example.

455   Warhaftig, Itamar. "The Ethics of Using Prisoners for Experimentation." *Techumin: Torah, Society, and State: Compendium of Halakha* 1 (1980): 530-536.

See the annotation at entry 406.

THE RIGHT TO LIFE

456   Bar-Zev, Asher. "Euthanasia:A Classical Ethical Problem in a Modern Context." *Reconstructionist* 44, 9-10 (1979): 7-16, 7-10.

See the annotation at entry 045.

457   Bardfelt, Philip A. "Jewish Medical Ethics." *Reconstructionist* 42, 6 (1976): 7-11.

See the annotation at entry 046.

458   Bick, Etta, ed. "Pekuah Nefesh." In her *Judaic Sources of Human Rights*, 99-114. Tel Aviv: Israel-Diaspora Institute, 1987.

See the annotation at entry 004.

459   Bleich, J. David. "The Quinlan Case: A Jewish Perspective." In *Contemporary Jewish Ethics*, ed. Menahem Marc Kellner, 296-307.

David M. L. Olivestone, series ed., Sanhedrin Jewish Studies. New York: Sanhedrin, 1978.

Bleich contends that Jewish morality is distinctive from that of American pragmatism. Whereas the former makes life primary, the latter makes individualism central.

460   Blidstein, Gerald J. "Moral Generalizations and Halakhic Discourse." *S'vara: A Journal of Philosophy and Judaism* 1, 2 (1991): 8-12.

See the annotation at entry 175.

461   Carmi, Amnon. "To Live Like A King: Die Like A King." In his *Law and Medicine*, 28-63. Haifa: Tamar, 1987.

See the annotation at entry 063.

462   Cohn, Haim H. "On the Meaning of Human Dignity." *Israel Yearbook on Human Rights* 13 (1983): 226-251

See the annotation at entry 199.

463   Dagi, Teodoro Forcht. "The Paradox of Euthanasia." *Judaism* 24 (1975): 157-167.

Dagi asks who is ultimately responsible for death--the physician or God. Since some interference with nature is permitted the question of when that interference is prohibited is difficult to answer.

464   Daube, David. "The Rabbis and Philo on Human Rights." In *Human Rights in Essays on Human Rights: Contemporary Issues and Jewish Perspectives*, ed. David Sidorsky, *et al.*, 234-246. Philadelphia: Jewish Publication Society, 1979.

See the annotation at entry 071.

465   Freehof, Solomon B. "Allowing a Terminal Patient to Die." In his *Modern Reform Responsa*, 197-203. Cincinnati: Hebrew Union College Press, 1971.

Freehof declares that the attending physician must have complete autonomy. Where there is a chance for life, Judaism demands treatment. The view represents the application of the principle that human beings have an unalienable right to life.

466   Freehof, Solomon B. "Determination and Postponement of Death." In his *Modern Reform Responsa*, 188-197. Cincinnati: Hebrew Union College Press, 1971.

Freehof discusses the classic problem of determining the moment of death. He notes the prohibition against hastening death as well as the permission to allow death to take its course. Here he implies a right to dignified death as a basic human right.

467   Freehof, Solomon B. "Relieving Pain of a Dying Patient." In his *Reform Responsa for Our Time*, 84-89. Cincinnati: Hebrew Union College Press, 1971.

Freehof looks at the question in the light of discussions of suicide in Judaism. He contends that Jewish law recognizes the pain that motivates both suicide and euthanasia even while discouraging such actions. This responsa reflects an inherent right to dignity and minimization of pain.

468   Greenberg, Hayyim. "The Right to Kill?" In *Jewish Reflections on Death*, ed. Jack Reimer, 107-116. New York: Schocken, 1974.

Greenberg emphasizes the primacy of life. He suggests that euthanasia puts the selfish personal desires of the patient before the principle of life. The right for life, in his view, takes precedence over such private concerns.

469   Halevi, Chaim David. "Disconnecting a Terminal Patient From an Artificial Respirator." *Techumin: Torah, Society, and State: Compendium of Halakha* 2 (1981): 297-305.

The author reviews relevant data on euthanasia including the stages of dying, the prohibition on hastening death and the permissibility of removing of obstacles. He does not discuss a right to a dignified death but implies the rejection of such a right.

470   Halibard, G. B. "Euthanasia." *Jewish Law Annual* 1 (1978): 196-199.

Halibard reviews the criteria used in deciding to end life. He discusses the motivation for such an action and the definition of taking one's own life both of which are important considerations in determining a right to a dignified death.

471   Herring, Basil F. "Euthanasia." In his *Jewish Ethics and Halakhah For Our Time: Sources and Commentary*, 67-90. Library of Jewish Law and Ethics 11. New York: Ktav, 1984.

Herring summarizes the major traditional arguments against euthanasia including an emphasis on the primacy of life which suggests a human right to life in contrast to a right to a dignified death.

472   Heschel, Abraham Joshua. "The Patient as Person." In his *The Insecurity of Freedom: Essays on Human Existence*, 24-38. New York: Schocken, 1972.

See the annotation at entry 090.

473   Jakobovits, Yoel. "Neonatal Euthanasia:Jewish Views of a Contemporary Dilemma." *Tradition* 22, 3 (1986): 13-30.

Jakobovits reviews the major themes and differences between prolonging life and preventing death. Again it is clear that according to traditional Jewish law human beings have no clear right to death.

474   Katz, Nathan. "Jewish Perspectives on Equality." *Ethnic Studies Report* IV, 1 (January 1986): 64-70.

See the annotation at entry 099.

475   Klein, Isaac. "Euthanasia: A Jewish View." In *Perspectives On Jews and Judaism: Essays in Honor of Wolfe Kelman*, ed. Arthur A. Chiel, 249-255. New York: Rabbinical Assembly, 1978.

Klein emphasizes the primacy of life and God as the sole arbiter of that life. He notes both the obligation to heal and the permission to allow nature to take its course rather than prolong pain. He discusses the relevance of 'brain death' to halakha.   While not mentioning either a 'right' to life or to death, the theory of such rights clearly informs this essay.

476   Novak, David. "Euthanasia in Jewish Law." In his *Law and Theology in Judaism*, 98-117. New York: Ktav, 1976.

Novak reviews the major concerns Jewish tradition has with euthanasia. While Jewish compassion recognizes the need to deal with a patient's suffering, compassion never involves a direct action to terminate a life.

477   Polish, Daniel F. "Judaism and Human Rights." In *Human Rights in Religious Traditions*, ed. Arlene Swidler, 40-50. New York: Pilgrim, 1982.

See the annotation at entry 117.

478   Rackman, Emanuel. "Medical-Legal Problems." In his *One Man's Judaism*, 107-119. New York: Philosophical Library, 1971.

See the annotation at entry 412.

479   Rosner, Fred. "The Jewish Attitude Toward Euthanasia." In *Jewish Bioethics*, eds. Fred Rosner and J. David Bleich, 255-265. David M. L. Olivestone, series ed., Sanhedrin Jewish Studies. New York: Sanhedrin, 1979.

See the annotation at entry 123.

480   Rosner, Fred. "The Use and Abuse of Heroic Measures to Prolong Dying." *Journal of Religion and Health* 17 (1978): 8-18.

Rosner notes recent cases that argue for a right to a dignified death and deplores the slogans that cloud the real question. He suggests that Jewish and Christian values are dramatically different towards this issue, particularly in their orientation to the human right to life as opposed to the duty to live.

481   Roth, Sol. "Human Rights." In his *Halakhah and Politics: The Jewish Idea of the State*, 117-128. Norman Lamm, series ed., The Library of Jewish Law and Ethics 14. Hoboken, NJ: Ktav, 1988.

See the annotation at entry 283.

482   Shapira, Amos. "Human Right to Die: Israeli and Jewish Legal Perspectives." *Israel Yearbook on Human Rights* 7 (1977): 127-138.

See the annotation at entry 127.

483   Sherwin, Byron L. "Jewish Views on Euthanasia." *Humanist* 34, 4 (1974): 19-21.

See the annotation at entry 129.

484   Sherwin, Byron L. "To Be Or...A Jewish View of Euthanasia." *United Synagogue Review* 25, 1 (1972): 4-5.

See the annotation at entry 131.

485   Sherwin, Byron L. "A View of Euthanasia." *Journal of Aging and Judaism* 2, 1 (1987): 35-57.

See the annotation at entry 132.

486   Shnit, Dan. "The Foetus as a Legal Person Under Israeli Law." *Israel Yearbook on Human Rights* 16 (1986): 308-320.

The author understands the claim that the foetus is not deemed to be a person capable of having rights but notes that this view is quite different from the position discernable in decisions of United States courts. He notes as well that Israeli law does not recognize a claim based on negligent infliction of harm to the foetus.

487   Silver, Daniel Jeremy. "The Right to Die." In *Jewish Reflections on Death*, ed. Jack Reimer, 117-125. New York: Schocken, 1975.

See the annotation at entry 134.

488   Warhaftig, Itamar. "The Ethics of Using Prisoners for Experimentation." *Techumin: Torah, Society, and State: Compendium of Halakha* 1 (1980): 530-536.

See the annotation at entry 406.

489   Weinberger, Yaakov. "Euthanasia in Jewish Religious Law." *Dine Israel* (1976): 99-117.

Weinberger notes that Judaism obligates treatment and rejects the idea of a living will for the termination of treatment. He recounts the traditional expectation for a physician's duties. He notes that Judaism takes account of the patient's condition in its decisions.

490   Weisbard, Alan J. "On the Bioethics of Jewish Law: The Case of Karen Quinlan." *Israel Law Review* 14 (1979): 337-368.

Weisbard summarizes the case of Karen Ann Quinlan and Jewish contributions to the debate, relying heavily on the work of J. David Bleich. He contends that a jury rather than a judge should decide cases of such moral weight.

THE RIGHTS OF MINORITIES

491   Agus, Irving A. "The Rights and Immunities of the Minority." *Jewish Quarterly Review, n.s.* 45 (1954-55): 120-129.

See the annotation at entry 149.

492   Beame, Abraham D. "Liberalism." *Judaism* (1972): 36-38.

See the annotation at entry 163.

493   Blum, Yehuda Z. "Reflections on the Changing Concept of Self-Determination." *Israel Law Review* 10, 4 (1975): 509-514.

This study looks at the way international law has understood the concept of self-determination and its particular relevance for Jews generally and for the state of Israel in its conflict with Arabs.

494   Cohn, Haim H. "Rights of Equality." In his *Human Rights in Jewish Law*, 149-186. New York: Ktav, 1984.

See the annotation at entry 357.

495   Gershuni, Jehudah. "Minority Rights in the State of Israel in the Light of Halacha." *Techumin: Torah, Society, and State: Compendium of Halakha* 2 (1981): 180-192.

See the annotation at entry 437.

496   Herzog, Yitzhak Isaac HaLevi. "Minority Rights According to Halacha." *Techumin: Torah, Society, and State: Compendium of Halakha* 2 (1981): 169-79.

See the annotation at entry 362.

497   Heschel, Abraham Joshua. "A Declaration of Conscience." In his *The Insecurity of Freedom: Essays on Human Existence*, 274-284. New York: Schocken, 1972.

See the annotation at entry 087.

THE RIGHT TO PRIVACY

498   Belkin, Samuel. "The Community." In his *In His Image: The Jewish Philosophy of Man as Expressed in Rabbinic Tradition*, 117-133. Westport, CT: Greenwood, 1979.

See the annotation at entry 049.

499   Cohen, Alfred S. "Privacy: A Jewish Perspective." *Journal of Halakha and Contemporary Society* 1 (1980): 53-102.

See the annotation at entry 066.

500   Cohn, Haim H. "Israeli Law and the Rights of the Individual." *Congress Monthly* 45, 3 (1978): 14-17, 20-21.

See the annotation at entry 325.

501   Cohn, Haim H. "The Right to Privacy." In his *Human Rights in Jewish Law*, 64-67. New York: Ktav, 1984.

Cohn argues that Jewish tradition emphasizes the rights of the individual and the individual's family to freedom from invasion by communal bodies.

502   Gavison, Ruth. "The Rights to Privacy and Dignity." In *Human Rights in Israel: Articles in Memory of Judge Haman Shelah*, ed. Ann Swersky, 61-80. Tel Aviv: Edanim and Yediot Aharonot, 1988. Hebrew.

See the annotation at entry 215.

503   Lamm, Norman. "The Fourth Amendment and its Equivalent in the Halakha." *Judaism* 16 (1967): 300-312.

Lamm contends that the Halakha recognizes that personality is at stake in preserving human privacy. What American law came to slowly through an evolution of sensitivity, Jewish law had already anticipated. This essay is reprinted in entry 012, pp. 225-233.

504   Rackman, Emanuel. "Privacy in Judaism." *Midstream* 28, 7 (1983): 31-34.

Rackman notes that Judaism requires duties to be performed voluntarily and thus rejects a police state. Such a respect for private conscience does not contradict the permission to coerce someone to obey a commandment because that applies only when the threat of a coercion will effect the desired result.

505   Rakover, Nahum. "The Protection of Privacy in Jewish Law." *Israel Yearbook on Human Rights* 5 (1975): 169-80.

Rakover notes that the delineation of privacy as an independent right is of modern origin. Even the fourth amendment of the US constitution protects privacy only partially. He discusses the penalty of excommunication established against any person who, without prior authority opens correspondence addressed to another. He notes the limits of the duty of preserving secrecy and the relevance of these laws for eavesdropping and domestic privacy.

THE RIGHT TO FREEDOM FROM RACISM

506   Booth, William H. "Racism and Human Rights." In *Black Anti-Semitism and Jewish Racism*, 117-127. New York: Richard W. Baron, 1969.

    Booth points out the inaccuracies that led to false charges of antisemitism and argues for full investigation of a person, a cause, or a movement before advancing such a charge.

507   Cruse, Harold. "My Jewish Question and Theirs." In *Black Anti-Semitism and Jewish Racism*, 143-188. New York: Richard W. Baron, 1969.

    Cruse provides a vivid autobiographical review of how Jewish co-option can pervade the life of an American black. He shows that Jews, conditioned by their European experience, accept American discrimination or oppose it out of self-interest. Jews should not equate the refusal of American blacks refusal to accept those interests as their own with antisemitism. While blacks may understand the biases of American Jews, they should also be permitted their right to self-determination.

508   Heschel, Abraham Joshua. "Religion and Race." In his *The Insecurity of Freedom: Essays on Human Existence*, 85-100. New York: Schocken, 1972.

    See the annotation at entry 091.

509   Heschel, Abraham Joshua. "The White Man on Trial." In his *The Insecurity of Freedom: Essays on Human Existence*, 101-111. New York: Schocken, 1972.

    See the annotation at entry 094.

WAR AND THE RIGHT TO PEACE

510   Dorff, Elliot N. "Defensive War." *S'vara: A Journal of Philosophy and Judaism* 1, 2 (1991): 25-29.

    See the annotation at entry 072.

511   Gendler, Everett E. "War and the Jewish Tradition." In *Contemporary Jewish Ethics*, ed. Menahem M. Kellner, 189-210. David M. L. Olivestone, series ed., Sanhedrin Jewish Studies. New York: Sanhedrin, 1978.

    See the annotation at entry 330.

512   Greenberg, Moshe. "Rabbinic Reflections on Defying Illegal Orders:
      Amasa, Abner, and Joab." In *Contemporary Jewish Ethics*, ed.
      Menahem M. Kellner, 211-220.   David M. L. Olivestone, series
      ed., Sanhedrin Jewish Studies. New York: Sanhedrin, 1978.

      See the annotation at entry 082.

513   Lamm, Maurice. "After the War - Another Look at Pacifism and Selective
      Conscientious Objection (SCO)." In *Contemporary Jewish Ethics*,
      ed. Menahem M. Kellner, 221-238.   David M. L. Olivestone,
      series ed., Sanhedrin Jewish Studies. New York: Sanhedrin, 1978.

      See the annotation at entry 344.

514   Landman, Leo. "Law and Conscience: The Jewish View." *Judaism* 18
      (1969): 17-29.

      See the annotation at entry 107.

WELFARE RIGHTS

515   Carmi, Amnon. "No Treatment - No Compensation." In his *Law and
      Medicine*, 294-308. Haifa: Tamar, 1987.

      See the annotation at entry 410.

516   Goldmann, Alain. "Les Sources Juives des Droits de l'Homme." In
      Judaisme et Droits de l'Homme, ed. Emmanuel Hirsch, 45-51.
      Idéologies et Droits de l'Homme   B.01. Paris: Librairie des
      Libertés, 1984. French.

      See the annotation at entry 080.

517   Hirsch, Richard G. "There Shall Be No Poor." In *Judaism and Human
      Rights*, ed. Milton R. Konvitz, 234-246. New York: W. W. Norton,
      1972.

      Hirsch argues that since human life is sacred the life of the poor
      must be protected.   Jewish law includes demands for charity,
      restricts control over property, and requires interhuman justice. Laws
      help preserve the dignity of those receiving charity. Jews developed
      social mechanisms for aiding the poor. The right to property, then,
      seems to Hirsch, protected by Jewish law.

518   Kaplan, Mordecai M. *The Meaning of God in Jewish Religion*. New York: Reconstructionist, 1962.

See the annotation at entry 098.

519   Kohn, Eugene. "Human Rights vs. Property Rights in Jewish Law." *Reconstructionist* 1, 3 (1935): 7-14.

See the annotation at entry 243.

520   Levine, Aaron. *Economics and Jewish Law*. Norman Lamm, series ed., The Library of Jewish Law and Ethics   13. Hoboken, NJ and New York: Ktav and Yeshivah University Press, 1987.

See the annotation at entry 419.

521   Roth, Sol. "Human Rights." In his *Halakhah and Politics: The Jewish Idea of the State*, 117-128.   Norman Lamm, series ed., The Library of Jewish Law and Ethics   14. Hoboken, NJ: Ktav, 1988.

See the annotation at entry 283.

522   Walzer, Michael. "Security and Welfare." In his *Spheres of Justice: A Defense of Pluralism and Equality*, 63-83. New York: Basic Books, 1983.

Using ancient Athens and medieval Jewish life as examples, Walzer shows how communities have reallocated goods in accordance with a shared understanding of needs. The social contract turns out to be moderated by specific cultural decisions concerning values and social welfare that are not universal but determined by communal interpretations of the social union.

THE RIGHTS OF WOMEN

523   Ahroni, Reuben. "The Levirate and Human Rights." *Jewish Law and Current Legal Problems*, ed. Nahum Rakover, 67-76. Library of Jewish Law. Jerusalem: Jewish Legal Heritage Society, 1984.

See the annotation at entry 042.

524   Berman, Saul J. "The Status of Women in Halakhic Judaism." *Tradition* 1 (1973): 5-18.

See the annotation at entry 054.

525   Cohn, Haim H. "Discriminations of Women." In his *Human Rights in Jewish Law*, 167-177. New York: Ktav, 1984.

See the annotation at entry 067.

526   Fishbane, Michael. "The Image of the Human and the Rights of the Individual in Jewish Tradition." In *Human Rights and World's Religions*, ed. Leroy S. Rouner, 17-32.   Leroy S. Rouner, series ed.,   Boston University Studies in Philosophy and Religion 9. South Bend, IN: University of Notre Dame Press, 1988.

See the annotation at entry 076.

527   Goitein, S. D. "Human Rights in Jewish Thought and Life in the Middle Ages." In *Essays on Human Rights: Contemporary Issues and Jewish Perspectives*, eds. David Sidorsky, *et al.*, 247-264. Philadelphia: Jewish Publication Society, 1979.

See the annotation at entry 079.

528   Gugenheim, Claude-annie. "La Femme Dans la Loi Juive." In *Judaisme et Droits de l'Homme*, ed. Emmanuel Hirsch, 37-41.   Idéologies et Droits de l'Homme B.01. Paris: Librairie des Libertés, 1984. French.

According to the author, the status of women in Judaism challenges its claim to respect human rights. Women often find their rights to education, profession, and personal development thwarted.

529   Guttmann, Alexander. "The Role of Equity in the History of the Halakhah." In *Julius Mark Jubilee Volume*, eds. Ronald Sobel and Sidney Wallach, 71-92. New York: Ktav, 1975.

See the annotation at entry 083.

530   Keddie, Nikki R. "The Rights of Women in Contemporary Islam." In *Human Rights and World's Religions*, ed. Leroy S. Rouner, 76-110. Leroy S. Rouner, series ed.,   Boston University Studies in Philosophy and Religion 9. South Bend, IN: University of Notre Dame Press, 1988.

While focused on the Islamic view of woman's rights and the diversity of practice that results despite that view, the author mentions several times a parallel between the treatment of women in Judaism and certain practices found in some Muslim communities.

531   Kurzweil, Zvi. "Equality of Women." In his *The Modern Impulse of Traditional Judaism*, 117-123. Hoboken, NJ: Ktav, 1985.

Kurzweil insists that the fact of non-identical obligations for men and women does not necessarily constitute a breach of human rights. The Jewish ideal emphasizes equality between the sexes and advocates giving Jewish women their basic rights. Nevertheless, he notes that historical reality often impaired this ideal, although Jewish law has struggled to solve this contradiction of its basic values. He thinks that the resolution should be left to the good sense of the Jewish people.

532   Lahav, Pnina. "Status of Women in Israel: Myth and Reality." *American Journal of Comparative Law* 22, 1 (1974): 107-129.

Lahav notes the myth of the Israeli's woman's putative equality with men and the reality of her subordinate position. She suggests that the latter has connections with traditional Jewish views of the place of women in religious life. The practical realities of the condition of women in Israel leads the author to reconsider the specific religious teachings in Judaism concerning the appropriate roles for each gender.

533   Levy, Annette. "Les Droits de la Femme dans la Tradition Juive." In *Judaisme et Droits de l'Homme*, ed. Emmanuel Hirsch, 53-58. Idéologies et Droits de l'Homme   B.01. Paris: Librairie des Libertés, 1984. French.

See the annotation at entry 110.

534   Meron, Theodor. *Human Rights Law-Making in the United Nations: A Critique of Instruments and Process.* Oxford: Clarendon Press, 1986.

See the annotation at entry 371.

535   Plaskow, Judith. *Standing Again At Sinai: Judaism From a Feminist Perspective.* San Francisco: Harper and Row, 1990.

See the annotation at entry 373.

536   Radi, F. *Women's Rights.* Jerusalem: The Association for Civil Rights in Israel, 1989. Hebrew.

Radi explains the theoretical basis on which Jews could advocate supporting equal rights for women and the traditional views that restrict the rights women can enjoy. She notes that the modern state of Israel tries to balance these two views, but has not succeeded. The gap between Israeli theory and practice on the question of women's rights demands an investigation of the theoretical and religious basis for denying women equality.

537   Rosen-Zvi, Ariel. "The Place of the Woman in the Family in Jewish Law." In *Human Rights in Israel: Articles in Memory of Judge Haman Shelah*, ed. Ann Swersky, 109-151. Tel Aviv: Edanim and Yediot Aharonot, 1988. Hebrew.

See the annotation at entry 122.

5

Human Rights and Contemporary Judaism

538   "Symposium on Human Rights: Groups (Minority) Rights." *Israel Yearbook on Human Rights* 1 (1971): 393-418.

See annotation at entry 001.

539   Agi, Marc. "Judaisme et Droits de l'Homme." In *Judaisme et Droits de l'Homme*, ed. Emmanuel Hirsch, 3-21. Idéologies et Droits de l'Homme B.01. Paris: Librairie des Libertés, 1984. French.

See the annotation at entry 041.

540   Agi, Marc. *René Cassin: Fantassin des Droits de l'Homme*. Paris: Plon, 1979. French.

See the annotation at entry 148.

541   Agus, Jacob B. "Religious Liberty in Judaism." In *Religious Liberty and Human Rights in Nations and in Religions*, ed. Leonard Swidler, 167-174. Philadelphia and New York: Ecumenical Press and Hippocrene Books, 1986.

See the annotation at entry 150.

542   Altmann, Alexander. "Moses Mendelssohn as the Archetypal German Jew." In *The Jewish Response to German Culture From the Enlightenment to the Second World War*, eds. Jehuda Reinharz and Walter Schatzberg, 17-31. Hanover, NH: University Press of New England, 1985.

See the annotation at entry 152.

543   Andrew, Edward. *Shylock's Rights: A Grammar of Lockian Rights.* Toronto: University Press of Toronto Press, 1988.

See the annotation at entry 153.

544   Artz, Donna E. and Liskofsky, Sidney. "Incitement to National, Racial and Religious Hatred in United Nations' Forums." *Israel Yearbook on Human Rights* 17 (1987): 41-67.

The authors argue that the rhetoric ostensibly related to Israel and Zionism suggests that Jews as a group cannot govern a legitimate government. While the United Nations usually welcomes national quests for self-determination, that of the Jews is singled out for hostility. As such that rhetoric represents antisemitism and by its very nature impairs the ideal of universal human rights.

545   Aschheim, Steven E. "Jew Within: The Myth of 'Judaization' in Germany." In *The Jewish Response to German Culture From the Enlightenment to the Second World War*, eds. Jehuda Reinharz and Walter Schatzberg, 212-241. Hanover, NH: University Press of New England, 1985.

See the annotation at entry 154.

546   Avineri, Shlomo. "Marx and Jewish Emancipation." *Journal of the History of Ideas* 25 (1964): 445-450.

See the annotation at entry 156.

547   Baldwin, James. "Negroes Are Anti-Semitic Because They Are Anti-White?" In *Black Anti-Semitism and Jewish Racism*, 3-12. New York: Richard W. Baron, 1969.

Baldwin notes that all racism perplexes him. He suggests that both antisemitism and the oppression of blacks in America represent a challenge to America's perceived way of life. The question of racism applies not only to Jews or blacks but to all Americans.

548   Bar Navi, Eli. "Civil Rights--a Historical Perspective." In *Human Rights in Israel: Articles in Memory of Judge Haman Shelah*, ed. Ann Swersky, 11-21. Tel Aviv: Edanim and Yediot Aharonot, 1988. Hebrew.

See the annotation at entry 044.

549   Baron, Salo W. "The Evolution of Equal Rights: Civil and Political." *Essays on Human Rights: Contemporary Issues and Jewish*

Perspectives, eds. Sidorsky, *et al.*, 267-281. Philadelphia: Jewish Publication Society, 1979.

See the annotation at entry 160.

550   Ben-Israel, Ruth. "Is the Right to Strike A Collective Human Right?" *Israel Yearbook on Human Rights* 11 (1981): 195-216.

See the annotation at entry 415.

551   Bennett, William J. "Religious Belief and the Constitutional Order." In *Religious Beliefs, Human Rights, and the Moral Foundation of Western Democracy: 1986 Paine Lectures*, ed. Carl H. Esbeck, 1-11. Columbia, MO: University of Missouri-Columbia Press, 1986.

Referring to the Jewish congregations who celebrated George Washington's inauguration as President of the United States, Bennett claims that America is not a "Christian Sparta" but a "Judeo-Christian" nation whose civic values are rooted in the Jewish and Christian traditions.

552   Berinson, Zvi. "Freedom of Religion and Conscience in the State of Israel." *Israel Yearbook on Human Rights* 3 (1973): 223-232.

See the annotation at entry 320.

553   Bialik, Hayym Nahman. *Divrei Sifrut (Literary Essays)*. Tel Aviv: Devir, 1964. Hebrew.

See the annotation at entry 168.

554   Bick, Etta, ed. *Judaic Sources of Human Rights*. Tel Aviv: Israel-Diaspora Institute, 1987.

See the annotation at entry 003.

555   Bick, Etta, ed. "Sheat Hadechak." In her *Judaic Sources of Human Rights*, 16-44. Tel Aviv: Israel-Diaspora Institute, 1987.

See the annotation at entry 169.

556   Bieber, Hans-Joachim. "Anti-semitism as a Reflection of Social, Economic and Political Tension in Germany: 1880-1933." In *Jews and Germans From 1860-1933: The Problematic Symbiosis*, ed. David Bronsen, 33-77. Heidelberg: Carl Winter, 1979.

See the annotation at entry 353.

557   Blaustein, Albert. "Contemporary Trends in Constitution-Writing." In *Constitutionalism: The Israeli and American Experiences*, ed. Daniel J. Elazar, 171-177. Lanham, MD: University Press of America, 1990.

See the annotation at entry 056.

558   Blaustein, Jacob. *Human Rights: A Challenge to the United Nations and to Our Generation.* np: np, 1963.

This printed version of the "Dag Hammarskjold Memorial Lecture" emphasizes that the modern concern for human rights arose in reaction to the Nazi genocide of six million Jews. Blaustein calls for a move from affirming human rights to seeing their implementation.

559   Blum, Yehuda Z. "Reflections on the Changing Concept of Self-Determination." *Israel Law Review* 10, 4 (1975): 509-514.

See the annotation at entry 493.

560   Boim, Leon. "The National-Territorial Rights of the Jewish National Minority in the Soviet Union." *Israel Yearbook on Human Rights* 6 (1976): 239-251.

The attempt to create a national autonomous district for Jews has failed. The Soviets never granted the rights enumerated to these districts and used the districts only for the sake of propaganda. Their discrimination appears in the attempt to blame the Jews rather than the Soviet system for the failure of the effort to create such districts.

561   Booth, William H. "Racism and Human Rights." In *Black Anti-Semitism and Jewish Racism*, 117-127. New York: Richard W. Baron, 1969.

See the annotation at entry 506.

562   Borochov, Ber. "Facing Reality." In his *Nationalism and the Class Struggle: A Marxian Approach to the Jewish Problem, Selected Writings by Ber Borochov*, 89-93. New York: Young Poalei Zion Alliance of America, 1937.

See the annotation at entry 177.

563   Borowitz, Eugene B. "Freedom: The Metamorphoses of a Jewish Value." In his *Exploring Jewish Ethics: Papers on Covenant Responsibility*, 289-294. Detroit, MI: Wayne State University Press, 1990.

See the annotation at entry 179.

564   Borowitz, Eugene B. "Rethinking the Reform Jewish Theory of Social
       Action." *Journal of Reform Judaism* 27 (1980): 1-19.

See the annotation at entry 180.

565   Borowitz, Eugene B. "Social Justice, the Liberal Jewish Case." In his
       Exploring Jewish Ethics: Papers on Covenant Responsibility,
       295-307. Detroit, MI: Wayne State University Press, 1990.

See the annotation at entry 060.

566   Borowitz, Eugene B. "The Torah, Written and Oral, and Human Rights:
       Foundations and Deficiencies." In *The Ethics of World Religions and
       Human Rights*, eds. Hans Küng and Jürgen Moltmann, 25-33.
       London: SCM, 1990.

See the annotation at entry 061.

567   Calef, Michel. "Un Regard Juif sur l'Ambiguite des Droits de l'Homme."
       In *Judaisme et Droits de l'Homme*, ed. Emmanuel Hirsch, 133-160.
       Idéologies et Droits de l'Homme   B.01. Paris: Librairie des
       Libertés, 1984. French.

See the annotation at entry 189.

568   Cantor, Norman L. "On Clear and Present Danger, Clear Probability, and
       Free Speech Standards in Israel." *Israel Yearbook on Human Rights*
       16 (1986): 260-290.

See the annotation at entry 386.

569   Carey, Henry F., and Carey, John. "Hostility in United Nations Bodies to
       Judaism, the Jewish People and Jews as Such." *Israel Yearbook on
       Human Rights* 17 (1987): 29-40.

       The authors claim that apparently theological or political hostility to
       Judaism or to the State of Israel actually constitute antisemitism.
       Denunciations of the theological idea that Jews are a chosen people
       actually aim at destroying the Jews as a viable modern people.
       Claims Jewish religion makes the Jews unfit for ruling a nation-state
       are, in the view of these authors, antisemitic slurs against the 'Jewish
       character.' While disguised as either theology or sociological studies
       of Jewish readiness for statehood, these attacks are intended to deny
       Jews the right to self-government in their own homeland.

570   Carlebach, Julius. *Karl Marx and the Radical Critique of Judaism.* London: Kegan Paul, 1978.

See the annotation at entry 190.

571   Cassin, René. "From the Ten Commandments to the Rights of Man." In *Of Law and Man: Essays in Honor of Haim Cohn*, ed. Shlomo Shoham, 13-25. New York: Sabra, 1971.

See the annotation in entry 065.

572   Chafets, Zeev. "Press and Government in Israel." *Israel Yearbook on Human Rights* 14 (1984): 134-17.

See the annotation at entry 388.

573   Cohn, Haim H. "Discrimination of Jewish Minorities in Arab Countries." *Israel Yearbook on Human Rights* 1 (1971): 127-133.

See the annotation at entry 195.

574   Cohn, Haim H. "Israeli Law and the Rights of the Individual." *Congress Monthly* 45, 3 (1978): 14-17, 20-21.

See the annotation at entry 325.

575   Coleman, Howard D. "The Problem of Anti-Semitism Under the International Convention on the Elimination of All Forms of Racial Discrimination." *Revue des Droits de l'Homme.   Human Rights Journal* 2, 4 (1969): 609-631.

This article studies the absence of an explicit reference to antisemitism in the International Convention on the Elimination of All Forms of Racial Discrimination and wonders whether Jews are being granted their right of equality of treatment and whether the Convention itself may display antisemitism.

576   Cruse, Harold. "My Jewish Question and Theirs." In *Black Anti-Semitism and Jewish Racism*, 143-188. New York: Richard W. Baron, 1969.

See the annotation at entry 507.

577   Dershowitz, Alan. "Due Process of Law in the Trial of Soviet Jews." *Israel Yearbook on Human Rights* 4 (1974): 253-265.

This discussion of the Jews in the Soviet Union argues that they have been deprived of human rights. Dershowitz contends that these Jews have been denied their rights to counsel, to present a defense, and to humane treatment under confinement.

578   Dershowitz, Alan. "Preventive Detention on Citizens During a National Emergency: A Comparison Between Israel and United States." *Israel Yearbook on Human Rights* 1 (1975): 295-321.

The author shows how a study of Jewish response to a specific challenge raises more general considerations of human rights. Studying Israel's peculiar situation leads to reflection on the principles behind the protection of rights in emergency situations.

579   Dinstein, Yoram. "Anti-Semitism, Anti-Zionism and the United Nations." *Israel Yearbook on Human Rights* 17 (1987): 15-23.

The author considers the Zionism as Racism Resolution the low point among many disappointments associated with the United Nations. He traces a slippery slope leading from anti-Israelism, through anti-Zionism, to anti-semitism in the speeches given at the United Nations. He wonders why other delegates do not intervene on a point of order or why the presiding officer does not rule that speakers overstep permissible bounds.

580   Dinstein, Yoram. "Collective Human Rights of Peoples and Minorities." *International and Comparative Law Quarterly* 25, 1 (1976): 102-120.

This article looks at the status of minorities and their rights to equal treatment with special reference to Israel and to Jews.

581   Dinstein, Yoram. "Derogation From International Human Rights." In *Menschenrechte in Israel und Deutschland: Ein Syumposium der Gesellschaft Zür Forderung der Wissenschaftlichen Zusammenarbeit mit der Universitat Tel Aviv (Human Rights in Israel and Germany: A Symposium of the Society for the Advancement of Scientific Cooperation with Tel Aviv University)*, ed. Gustav Stein, 63-71. Cologne: Nottbeck, 1978.

This essay studies the modern international situation, with special reference to the state of Israel, and problems with defining both international human rights and conditions that call for their suspension.

582   Dinstein, Yoram. "Discrimination and International Human Rights." *Israel Yearbook on Human Rights* 15 (1985): 11-17.

See the annotation at entry 326.

583   Dinstein, Yoram. "Freedom of Emigration and Soviet Jewry." *Israel Yearbook on Human Rights* 4 (1974): 266-274.

The author claims that while not an absolute right, the freedom to short-term departures from one's country and to emigration are a human right. Certain general qualifications apply, but they are not germane to the case of Soviet Jews. He concludes that the right is of importance since in the field of human rights every human individual counts.

584   Dinstein, Yoram. "Human Rights: The Quest for Concretization." *Israel Yearbook on Human Rights* 1 (1971): 12-28.

Even a vague list of human rights classified by subgroups engenders controversy. The author notes that Jews perhaps more than others have learned the probability that freedom of religion is the most persistently violated right. He notes the general agreement on the right to marriage and its practical abridgement in Israel. The author maintains that this problem of concretization should not be present within the UN.

585   Dinstein, Yoram. "The International Human Rights of Soviet Jews," *Israel Yearbook on Human Rights* 2 (1972): 194-210.

The author notes that the Jewish struggle is not merely a struggle for Jews but for equality of deprivation: whatever the deprivation of human rights in the USSR, it should at least apply to all Soviet citizens. The human right that is involved is that of freedom from discrimination. Jews, not merely as a minority, but as a special minority, suffer ethnic, religious, and linguistic disadvantages. This essay revised as "Soviet Jewry and International Rights" is also found in entry 020, pp. 126-143.

586   Dinstein, Yoram. "Terrorism and Wars of Liberation Applied to the Arab-Israeli Conflict: An Israeli Perspective." *Israel Yearbook on Human Rights* 3 (1973): 78-92.

While admitting the right of self-determination for a people, the author points to the difficulty in deciding when a group becomes one. The test of Arab legalism must be the response to terrorism which runs from accepting it, tolerating it, or seeking to fit it.

587   Elazar, Daniel J., ed. *Constitutionalism: The Israeli and American Experiences.* Lanham, MD: University Press of America, 1990.

See the annotation at entry 007.

588   Elazar, Daniel J. "Constitution-Making: The Pre-Eminently Political Act."
       In his *Constitutionalism: The Israeli and American Experiences*,
       3-29. Lanham, MD: University Press of America, 1990.

       See the annotation at entry 204.

589   Elazar, Daniel J. "Preface." In his *Constitutionalism: The Israeli and
       American Experiences*, xi-xv. Lanham, MD: University Press of
       America, 1990.

       See the annotation at entry 205.

590   Enker, Arnold. "The Issue of Religion in the Israeli Supreme Court." In
       *The Constitutional Bases of Political and Social Change in the
       United States*, ed. Shlomo Slonim, 314-317. Westport, CT: Praeger,
       1990.

       Enker argues that merely because certain legislation is religious or
       promotes religious interests does not argue against its validity. Local
       regulations, he notes, often do not accommodate as broad a range of
       interests as does national legislation. He illustrates this distinction
       by referring to a controversy over the commemoration of the Jewish
       day of mourning, the Ninth of Av, on which one Israeli municipality
       legislated the closing of restaurants and places of entertainment.
       While the national law did not require such legislation, was the
       municipal law valid? It was held to be so since it upheld a
       reasonable accommodation of all substantial interests.

591   Esbeck, Carl H. *Religious Beliefs, Human Rights, and the Moral
       Foundation of Western Democracy: 1986 Paine Lectures*. Columbia,
       MO: University of Missouri-Columbia Press, 1986.

       See the annotation at entry 008.

592   Falk, Zeev W. "Human Rights." In his *Law and Religion: The Jewish
       Experience*, 75-89. Jerusalem: Mesharim, 1981. Hebrew.

       See the annotation at entry 073.

593   Foxman, Abraham H. "Anti-semitism in the United States." In
       Anti-Semitism and Human Rights, ed. Serge Liberman, 19-26. North
       Melbourne, Vic.: Australian Institute of Jewish Affairs, 1985.

       See the annotation at entry 212.

594   Friedlander, Henry. "The Holocaust, Anti-Semitism and the Jewish
       Catastrophe." In *The Study of Judaism: Bibliographical Essays*,
       207-229. New York: Ktav, 1972.

This survey and analysis shows how the Nazi experience draws attention to the precarious status of human rights in the modern nation state.

595   Friedman, Saul S. *Pogromchik: The Assassination of Simon Petlura.* New York: Hart, 1976.

In the guise of a study of Sholom Schwartzbard's 1926 assassination of the Ukrainian hero Simon Petular and his ensuing trial and acquittal, Friedman studies how antisemitic pogroms stir the world conscience. He notes the rhetoric of human rights but concludes that this rhetoric often hides procrastination, retribution, or an empty liberalism. Instead of these maneuvers, he advocates an active commitment to justice and love.

596   Gavison, Ruth. *Civil Rights and Democracy.* Jerusalem: The Association for Civil Rights in Israel, 1988. Hebrew.

See the annotation at entry 327.

597   Gavison, Ruth. "The Controversy Over Israel's Bill of Rights." *Israel Yearbook on Human Rights* 15 (1985): 113-154.

See the annotation at entry 328.

598   Gavison, Ruth. "Introduction." In her *Civil Rights in Israel,* 9-46. Jerusalem: The Association for Civil Rights in Israel, 1982. Hebrew.

See the annotation at entry 329.

599   Gavison, Ruth. "The Rights to Privacy and Dignity." In *Human Rights in Israel: Articles in Memory of Judge Haman Shelah,* ed. Ann Swersky, 61-80. Tel Aviv: Edanim and Yediot Aharonot, 1988. Hebrew.

See the annotation at entry 215.

600   Genn, Rowel. "Beyond the Pale: Council of Europe Measures Against Incitement to Hatred." *Israel Yearbook on Human Rights* 13 (1983): 189-207.

The author considers the declaration of human rights part of a many sided opposition to resurgent Nazism. He places an emphasis on the duty to oppose hatred owed not merely toward the individual or group offended but toward democracy as a whole.

601 Gershuni, Jehudah. "Minority Rights in the State of Israel in the Light of Halacha." *Techumin: Torah, Society, and State: Compendium of Halakha* 2 (1981): 180-192.

See the annotation at entry 437.

602 Gerson, Allan. "The United Nations and Anti-Semitism." In *Anti-Semitism and Human Rights*, ed. Serge Liberman, 53-56. North Melbourne, Vic.: Australian Institute of Jewish Affairs, 1985.

Focusing on the anti-semitism of the United Nations, Alan Gerson shows how the United Nations has attempted to delegitimize Judaism and the State of Israel, thereby making a mockery of its proclamation of human rights.

603 Gerson, Allan. "The United Nations and Racism: The Case for the Zionism as Racism Resolution as Progenitor." *Israel Yearbook on Human Rights* 17 (1987): 68-73.

The author claims that this declaration serves to legitimate terrorism not only against Israel's citizens, but against the State itself. Ironically, he concludes that anti-Zionism and all it engenders is the very antithesis and abnegation of the UN charter.

604 Gilman, Sander. "Karl Marx and the Secret Language of Jews." *Modern Judaism* 4, 3 (1984): 275-294.

See the annotation at entry 216.

605 Glahn, Gerhard von. "The Protection of Human Rights in Time of Armed Conflict." *Israel Yearbook on Human Rights* 1 (1971): 208-227.

This essay studies the importance of protecting human rights even during a time of war. The contemporary references in this essay make it relevant to understanding the Israeli treatment of Muslim Arabs.

606 Glazer, Nathan. "Individual Rights Against Group Rights." In *Human Rights*, eds. Eugene Kamenka and Alice Erh-Soon Tay, 87-103. London: Edward Arnold, 1978.

Glazer focuses on the text case of rights in the United States and in particular on the Civil Rights Act of 1964. He devotes considerable attention to the case of the Jews in America and notes that America fosters two traditions--one which insists on a unitary national identity and another which argues for cultural pluralism. He argues, against others, that for an American society in which people share a common identity and maintain subgroup identities as private choices.

He sees his stand as advocating individual rights rather than group rights.

607   Green, Leslie C. "Aspects Juridiques du Procès Eichmann." *Annuaire Français de Droit International 1963* 9 (1964): 150-190.

The idea of a universal right to life and the necessity to protect that right underlies this article. The author studies the responsibility for acts committed under government orders as exemplified in the Eichmann trial.

608   Green, Leslie C. "Human Rights and Law of Armed Conflict." *Israel Yearbook on Human Rights* 10 (1980): 9-37.

The author applies the theory of human rights to contemporary international situations, including that of the Arab-Israeli conflict.

609   Green, Leslie C. "Jewish Issues on the Human-Rights Agenda in the First Half of The Twentieth Century." In *Essays on Human Rights: Contemporary Issues and Jewish Perspectives*, eds., David Sidorsky, *et al.*, 297-308. Philadelphia: Jewish Publication Society, 1979.

Green suggests the new direction that Zionism advanced for the achievement of human rights. He notes that the Jewish response to the Kishnev pogroms emphasized the universal concern that the persecutions should awaken. He considers Israel's law of return actually a declaration of the right of asylum.

610   Green, Leslie C. "Terrorism and Armed Conflict: The Plea and the Verdict." *Israel Yearbook on Human Rights* 19 (1989): 131-166.

Green provides a wide-ranging survey of incidents in which acts of terrorism are defended as legitimate actions by combatants against a well defined enemy of war. Among the examples, Green points to cases in which PLO terrorism could be construed as war efforts by combatants. The response of Benjamin Rubin makes this essay of particular relevance.

611   Green, Leslie C. "War Crimes, Extradition, and Command Responsibility." *Israel Yearbook on Human Rights* 14 (1984): 17-53.

Green explores the general questions of extradition. When do laws of war apply? Does an incursion against 'terrorists' constitute a war and are offenses carried out by subordinates in such a conflict signs of the commander's implication? What about actions done by a 'friendly force' with the consent of the generals fighting? His focus is on the massacres at the refugee camps at Shatila and Sabra, Lebanon, September 1982.

612   Green Leslie C. "Self-determination and the Settlement of the Arab-Israeli Conflict." *American Journal of International Law* 65, 4 (1971): 40-48.

This essay applies the theory of human rights to various aspects of the Arab-Israeli conflict.

613   Greenspahn, Morris. "The Protection of Human Rights in Time of Warfare." *Israel Yearbook on Human Rights* 1 (1971): 228-245.

Modern experience, including that of Jews in the Middle East, provide a testing ground for the protection of human rights during war.

614   Gross, George M. "The Constitutional Question in Israel." In *Constitutionalism: The Israeli and American Experiences*, ed. Daniel J. Elazar, 51-86. Lanham, MD: University Press of America, 1990.

The author notes the basic rights enumerated in Israel's declaration of independence, the development and adaptation of constitutional laws, and the irony of French political thinkers advocating a Burkean approach to revision of the present constitutional system. He summarizes constitutional debates in Israel beginning in 1950 and notes the religious dimension in those debates.

615   Gross, Joseph. "The Right of Incorporation." *Israel Yearbook on Human Rights* 2 (1972): 277-286.

Gross notes that modern theory considers this an inherent right and not merely one granted by the state. The right is related to the right of freedom of association, although no such right is recognized for professional persons. He uses examples from contemporary Israeli experience to illustrate his contention.

616   Halpern, Ben. "Jewish Nationalism: Self-Determination as a Human Right." In *Essays on Human Rights: Contemporary Issues and Jewish Perspectives*, eds. David Sidorsky, *et al.*, 309-335. Philadelphia: Jewish Publication Society, 1979.

See the annotation at entry 222.

617   Hashin, Mishael. "Israel's Heritage and Civil Law." In *Civil Rights in Israel*, ed. Ruth Gavison, 47-83. Jerusalem: The Association for Civil Rights in Israel, 1982. Hebrew.

The author analyzes the influence of Hebrew law on Israeli judicial procedure. While admitting the validity of allowing national culture to influence law, he discusses the problems of deciding the will of the Jewish people and the religious coercion that results from the dominance of halakhic Judaism in Israel.

618   Hassoun, Jacques. "Le Role du Kahal dans L'Education aux Droits de l'Homme." In *Judaisme et Droits de l'Homme*, ed. Emmanuel Hirsch, 119-125. Idéologies et Droits de l'Homme B.01. Paris: Librairie des Libertés, 1984. French.

See the annotation at entry 085.

619   Hauser, Rita E. "International Protection of Minorities and the Right of Self-Determination." *Israel Yearbook on Human Rights* 1 (1977): 92-102.

Looking at modern examples, the author analyzes both the right of minorities to protection and their right to self-determination.

620   Henkin, Louis. "National and International Perspectives in Racial Discrimination." *Revue des Droits de l'Homme. Human Rights Journal* 4, 2-3 (1971): 263-269.

This article does not focus specifically on Jews and Judaism. Nevertheless as a leading Jewish thinker on the issue of human rights Henkin's position deserves consideration. He explores the political as well as ideological basis for various definitions of racism and expressions of racism.

621   Hentoff, Nat. "Introduction." In *Black Anti-Semitism and Jewish Racism*, ix-xvii. New York: Richard W. Baron, 1969.

This anthology does not name a particular editor. Hentoff performs the functions of such an editor when he reviews the various essays in this volume. He suggests the dimensions of concern for human rights, for Jewish-Black relations, and the new American situation (after the teacher's strike in New York in 1968) that the several essays evince.

622   Herzog, Chaim. "Judaism, Law and Justice." *Israel Yearbook on Human Rights* 14 (1984): 9-16.

See the annotation at entry 225.

623   Herzog, Yitzhak Isaac HaLevi. "Minority Rights According to Halacha." *Techumin: Torah, Society, and State: Compendium of Halakha* 2 (1981): 169-79.

See the annotation at entry 362.

624   Heschel, Abraham Joshua. "A Declaration of Conscience." In his *The Insecurity of Freedom: Essays on Human Existence*, 274-284. New York: Schocken, 1972.

See the annotation at entry 087.

625   Heschel, Abraham Joshua. *The Insecurity of Freedom: Essays on Human Existence*. New York: Schocken, 1972.

See the annotation at entry 088.

626   Heschel, Abraham Joshua. "Jews in the Soviet Union." In his *The Insecurity of Freedom: Essays on Human Existence*, 262-273. New York: Schocken, 1972.

See the annotation at entry 089.

627   Higgins, Rosalyn. "Human Right of Soviet Jews to Leave: Violations and Obstacles." *Israel Yearbook on Human Rights* 4 (1974): 275-287.

Higgins claims that the large number of Jews who wish to emigrate testifies to the lack of human rights granted to the minority group involved. She notes that the right to emigrate is itself a cluster of rights to freedom of movement.

628   Israel, Gerard. *The Jews in Russia*. Trans. Sanford L. Chernoff. New York: St Martin's, 1973.

This book traces the fate of Jews in Russia from the Tsarist regimes through Israel's six day war. It shows how the Jewish cause has stirred the concern of the world for human rights but also how that concern has always ebbed.

629   Jakobovits, Immanuel. "Anti-Semitism: After the Holocaust, After the State of Israel." In *Anti-Semitism and Human Rights*, ed. Serge Liberman, 1-6, 34-35. North Melbourne, Vic.: Australian Institute of Jewish Affairs, 1985.

See the annotation at entry 368.

630   Kaplan, Mordecai M. *The Future of the American Jew*. New York: MacMillan, 1948.

See the annotation at entry 235.

631   Kasher, Asa. "Justice and Affirmative Action: Naturalization and the Law of Return." *Israel Yearbook on Human Rights* 15 (1985): 101-112.

Kasher claims that justice plays a role even when the distinction between citizens and non-citizens applies. He argues that justice must encourage self-respect by avoiding the creation of social conditions that end to undermine it. He uses as his prime example the Israeli law of return that seems to invite a favoritism that infringes on both self-respect and the advantage of all citizens. Nevertheless, he defends the law as necessary for implementing the right to enjoy asylum from persecution. Kasher offers some suggestions of how to construe such a situation.

632   Katz, Jacob. "Post Emancipation Development of Rights: Liberalism and Universalism." In *Essays on Human Rights: Contemporary Issues and Jewish Perspectives*, ed. David Sidorsky, *et al.*, 282-296. Philadelphia: Jewish Publication Society, 1979.

Katz shows that Jews did not immediately welcome emancipation nor were they immediately accepted into the new emancipated states. Jews were drawn into the left-wing of society since change alone could allow them entrance into the society as a whole. This entrance into society led to antisemitism. He claims that the Jewish espousal of liberalism also had its roots in the system of Jewish thoughts and beliefs.

633   Katz, Jacob. "The Term 'Jewish Emancipation': Its Origin and Historical Impact." In *Studies in Nineteenth-Century Jewish Intellectual History*, ed., Alexander Altmann, 1-26. Cambridge, MA: Harvard University Press, 1964.

See the annotation at entry 238.

634   Keyes, Alan L. "Anti-Zionism, Anti-Semitism and the Decline of the UN Ideal." *Israel Yearbook on Human Rights* 17 (1987): 24-28.

Keyes explains the Soviet view of the UN as an ideological and geopolitical weapon and its use of the language of human rights. He concludes that much of the discussion of human rights in the United Nations conceals an antisemitic agenda.

635   Knisbacher, Mitchell. "Aliyah of Soviet Jews: Protection of the Right of Emigration Under International Law." *Harvard International Law Journal* 14, 1 (1973): 89-110.

This study looks at the obstacles placed before Soviet Jews in their attempt to leave the Soviet Union in the light of the right of emigration.

636   Knisbacher, Mitchell. "The Jews of Iraq (1956-1976): A Case Study of the International Protection of the Rights of Minorities." *International Yearbook on Human Rights* 6 (1976): 252-293.

The author describes how, after World War I, Jews were granted the status of an independent minority in Iraq. After the collapse of the League of Nations, however, they lost the protection of the international community. The Arab government of Iraq resented its forced acceptance of obligations to minorities, and, indeed, human rights guarantees deteriorated up to World War II. The predicament of such a condition is well illustrated by the pogroms that broke out against the Jews of Iraq after the passage of the United Nations' partition plan for Palestine. He concludes with the recognition that Jews as a minority enjoyed security only when Iraq was non-self-governing. The violation of the United Nations human rights conventions was blatant but unprotested. Thus while the United Nations has defined human rights it has not helped enforce their protection. This article is also found in entry 020, pp. 157-178.

637   Korey, William. "The 'Right to Leave' for Soviet Jews: Legal and Moral Aspects." *Soviet Jewish Affairs* 1 (1971): 5-12.

This study of the plight of Jews in the Soviet Union uses this situation to investigate the moral and legal aspects of the human right of movement.

638   Korey, William. "International Law and the Right to Study Hebrew in the USSR." *Soviet Jewish Affairs* 11, 1 (1981): 3-18.

The inequality of Jews in the Soviet Union is revealed by restrictions placed on the right to study Hebrew.

639   Korey, William. "The Triumph of Evil: UN Anti-Semitism." In
       Anti-Semitism and Human Rights, ed. Serge Liberman, 57-60. North
       Melbourne, Vic.: Australian Institute of Jewish Affairs, 1985.

       Using Edmund Burke's views on rights as a point of departure,
       Korey argues that people must respond to and refute the antisemitism
       of the United Nations. He notes that despite the commitment of the
       United Nations to the protection of human rights, delegates from the
       European, Canadian, and Latin American nations make no objection
       to antisemitic outpourings from Arab representatives.

640   Kretzmer, David. "The Influence of First Amendment Jurisprudence on
       Judicial Decision Making in Israel." In *The Constitutional Bases of
       Political and Social Change in the United States*, ed. Shlomo
       Slonim, 295-313. Westport, CT: Praeger, 1990.

       Kretzmer reviews Israeli use of the principle of freedom of speech,
       first generally, and then in terms of a specific case. He notes that
       the principle is fully integrated into the Israeli legal system. When
       ignoring the form of Israel's non-constitutional system, it is possible
       to see its reliance on United States precedent.

641   Lador-Lederer, J. Josef. *International Group Protection: Aims and Methods
       in Human Rights*. Leiden: Sijthoff, 1968.

       The author surveys treatment of minorities, including the treatment
       of Jewish minorities, and uses this as the basis for asserting the
       human right to equal treatment. Despite the different spelling of his
       name and initials this is the same author noted in the entries 642-645
       and indexed accordingly.

642   Lador-Lederer, Joseph H. "The Eichmann Case Revisited." *Israel Yearbook
       on Human Rights* 14 (1984): 54-79.

       The author deems it necessary to consider the experience of the
       victims when judging a criminal. He claims that crimes against
       humanity are independent of other crimes so that no single penalty
       can be applied in every case. He therefore defends the trial and
       sentence on Eichmann as a remedial post-conflict event meant to
       overcome the trauma of the war crimes themselves. It upholds
       human rights as an ideal even if in application the case seems to
       inflict extraordinary punishment.

643   Lador-Lederer, Joseph H. "The Lay Law on Religious Freedoms and the
       Canons of Response." *Israel Yearbook on Human Rights* 6 (1976):
       175-227.

Using Roman Catholicism as a test case, the author examines the relationship between espousing religious freedom and supporting human rights. The essay surveys the interaction between religious law in Roman Catholicism concerning religious freedom and lay law. The author notes that Jewish-Christian tension provides a subtext for this interaction. In contemporary life, he claims, as the lay law of religious freedoms extends into the international community, all religions will play equal roles.

644   Lador-Lederer, Josef J. "Refugee Care: The Jewish Case: Notes for an Analysis of the Status and Activity of Nongovernmental Organizations." *Israel Yearbook on Human Rights* 7 (1977): 77-126.

The author uses the case of Jewish refugees after World War II to examine the rights that should apply to such displaced persons.

645   Lador-Lederer, Joseph. "World War II: Jews as Prisoners of War." *Israel Yearbook on Human Rights* 10 (1980): 70-89.

The author contends that while treated politically as enemy combatants, Jews, during the Second World War, were not given the protection due to enemy prisoners of war. Since the German aim was the extinction of all Jews, those held in captivity represented an anomaly. They were not suffering the fortunes of war but enjoying a unique status. By 1941 this unique status became regularized as the Jews in the military camps suffered in ways not true for other prisoners. In the light of this evidence, the author concludes that international law itself on the treatment of prisoners demands rewriting.

646   Lahav, Pnina. "Status of Women in Israel: Myth and Reality." *American Journal of Comparative Law* 22, 1 (1974): 107-129.

See the annotation at entry 532.

647   Landau, Moshe. "The Limits of Constitutions and Judicial Review." In *Constitutionalism: The Israeli and American Experiences*, ed. Daniel J. Elazar, 197-205. Lanham, MD: University Press of America, 1990.

See the annotation at entry 106.

648   Laquer, Walter. "The Issue of Human Rights." In *Essays on Human Rights: Contemporary Issues and Jewish Perspectives*, David Sidorsky, *et al.*, 5-20. Philadelphia: Jewish Publication Society, 1979.

Laquer rejects the claim that the idea of universal human rights is a new invention. He notes, however, that the modern discussion focuses on economic and social as opposed to civil and political rights. He condemns the United Nations' Human Rights Commission for legitimizing a perversion of the idea of human rights and calls for a consistent application of a human rights standard. He demands that the United States respond to the challenge and create and enforce such a standard.

649   Laski, Neville Jonas. *Jewish Rights and Jewish Wrongs*. London: Soncino, 1939.

Laski's argument here suggests a peculiar view of human rights: they must be earned by the contributions a group makes to the general good and by their loyalty to the ideals of good citizenship. As a representative of the Board of Deputies of British Jews, his apologetic approach can be understood. Laski argues that Jews deserve human rights because of their contribution to world civilization. He recounts both Jewish contributions to Western culture and the victimization of Jews, especially by the Nazis. He sees his book as part of the effort by Jews to convince the general public that they are worthy of such rights. When touching on the question of a Jewish homeland in Israel he stresses the importance of granting equal rights to the Arabs.

650   Leibler, Isi. *Soviet Jewry and Human Rights*. Vic.: Human Rights Publications, n.d.

This study, released in 1964, was originally prepared for publication in a Marxist quarterly. It argues that the treatment of minorities such as the Jews in the Soviet Union tests the commitment of a society to the idea of human rights. It documents the violations of the human rights of Jews in the USSR and the contradiction between these violations and proclaimed Communist ideology.

651   Lerner, Natan. "Anti-Semitism as Racial and Religious Discrimination Under United Nations Conventions." *Israel Yearbook on Human Rights* 1 (1971): 103-115.

This study notes the lack of inclusion of antisemitism under United Nations conventions but also the obvious way in which antisemitism does fit into the definition of both racial and religious discrimination.

652   Lerner, Natan. "Group Libel Revisited." *Israel Yearbook on Human Rights* 17 (1987): 184-196.

Lerner argues that law is most effective when preventing not punishing crime. He thinks that legislation against group libel should include the possibility of redress once the offence is committed as well as provisions for preventing its commission.

653   Lerner, Natan. "Inter-group Tensions in Israel: Are Legal Solutions Effective?" *Israel Yearbook on Human Rights* 15 (1985): 88-100.

Lerner identifies four levels of concern about human rights in Israel: the status of the Jewish population and its inner divisions, relations to Arab minority, relations to weaker segments within the Jewish majority, and the status of women. He points to clashes between those legitimately entitled to benefit from affirmative action and reviews the issues of security, immigration, and the nature of the minorities which make the Israeli experience singular.

654   Lerner, Natan. "New Concepts in the Unesco Declaration on Race and Racial Prejudice." *Human Rights Quarterly* 3, 1 (1981): 48-61.

Lerner studies the hidden agenda within the definition of racial prejudice found in the Unesco declaration.

655   Lerner, Natan. *The UN Convention on the Elimination of All Forms of Racial Discrimination: a Commentary.* Leiden: Sijhoff, 1980.

This updates a 1970 study. Lerner reflects on the significance of the language of the UN Convention on the Elimination of All Forms of Racial Discrimination particularly in relationship to the Jews.

656   Levin, Shamarya. *The Arena.* Trans.   Maurice Samuel, New York: Harcourt Brace; Arno, 1932; 1975.

See the annotation at entry 251.

657   Levin, Stanley. "Due Process in Rabbinical and Israeli Law: Abuse and Subversion." In *Jewish Law and Current Legal Problems*, ed. Nahum Rakover, 191-194. Library of Jewish Law. Jerusalem: Jewish Legal Heritage Society, 1984.

See the annotation at entry 108.

658   Levinas, Emmanuel. "Nom D'Un Chien Ou Le Droit Naturel." In his *Difficile Liberté: Essais sur le Judaisme*, 187-202. Presences Du Judaisme. Paris: Albin Michel, 1963. French.

See the annotation at entry 254.

659   Levy, Annette. "Les Droits de la Femme dans la Tradition Juive." In
         Judaisme et Droits de l'Homme.   Emmanuel Hirsch, 53-58.
         Idéologies et Droits de l'Homme   B.01. Paris: Librairie des
         Libertés, 1984. French.

         See the annotation at entry 110.

660   Lew, M. S. *Jews and Human Rights.*   Jewish Topics of Today   11.
         London: World Jewish Congress, 1968.

         See the annotation at entry 111.

661   Lewin, Nathan. "Seeking Tolerance: Do Courts Respect Religious
         Observance?" In *The Constitutional Bases of Political and Social
         Change in the United States*, ed. Shlomo Slonim, 95-102. Westport,
         CT: Praeger, 1990.

         The author, an American lawyer, suggests that the modern period is
         one of intolerance to religious minorities. He gives examples of
         cases in which sabbath observers could not be protected under state
         law and in which an air force captain was compelled to go
         bareheaded despite his religious beliefs about wearing a skull cap.
         Problems arise when judges have no sympathy with the types of
         actions claimed as "religious." The author claims, however, that the
         First Amendment was meant to protect religious practice by religious
         minorities. Decisions that undermine that right to practice are
         encouraging intolerance.

662   Liberman, Serge, ed. *Anti-Semitism and Human Rights.* North Melbourne,
         Vic.: Australian Institute of Jewish Affairs, 1985.

         See the annotation at entry 013.

663   Liebeschutz, Hans. "German Radicalism and the Formation of Jewish
         Political Attitudes During the Earlier Part of the Nineteenth
         Century." In *Studies in Nineteenth-Century Jewish Intellectual
         History*, ed. Alexander Altmann, 141-170. Cambridge, MA: Harvard
         University Press, 1964.

         In the midst of discussing the formation of Jewish political attitudes
         the author reviews the controversies over granting rights to the Jews.
         He studies several of the supporters and opponents of such an act.

664   Lillich, Richard B. "Civil Rights." In *Human Rights in International Law:
         Legal and Policy Issues*, ed. Theodor Meron, 115-170. Oxford:
         Clarendon, 1984.

The author repeatedly turns to examples of Nazi misuse of law to demonstrate the difference between a civil law and the actions prescribed by the dictates of a civil right.

665   Liskofsky, Sidney, comp. *The United Nations and Human Rights -- What Are the Road Blocks: A Symposium.* New York: The American Jewish Committee, 1969.

See the annotation at entry 014.

666   Littman, David. *Human Rights and Human Wrongs.* New York: World Union for Progressive Judaism, 1986.

This statement rejects attempts to link Zionism with apartheid. It calls Zionism a struggle for human dignity and freedom. The author claims that the Zionist defense of Jewish nationalism never falls into the same racism as Muslim fundamentalism which encompasses a "grisly list of ideological hatred." He points to the oppression with which Muslims treated Jews historically to suggest that Jews suffered severe effects of colonialism over thousands of years. The author also calls attention to human rights violations against Jews by Arab countries and in the Soviet Union.

667   Litvinoff, Emanuel. "Russian Anti-Semitism: From Czar to Chernenko." In *Anti-Semitism and Human Rights*, ed. Serge Liberman, 61-73. North Melbourne, Vic.: Australian Institute of Jewish Affairs, 1985.

The author traces Russian antisemitism as an attempt to delegitimate the Jewish people. He claims that the global propaganda war by the Soviets against Jews has grave consequences for human rights throughout the world.

668   Loury, Glenn C. "Affirmative Action: Is It Just? Does It Work?" In *The Constitutional Bases of Political and Social Change in the United States*, ed. Shlomo Slonim, 109-139. Westport, CT: Praeger, 1990.

Loury points out that affirmative action can be defended for the wrong reasons. Preferential treatment of minorities, he suggests, must result from judgments arrived at through democratic process. It must express a commitment to accepted norms of human rights. Such treatment must reflect the norms of equality, not norms based on comparative judgments concerning a painful past or as payment for historical wrongs. He points to the mutual recriminations between blacks, emphasizing slavery, and Jews, emphasizing the holocaust, as examples of using norms based on presumed historical reasons rather than on human rights.

669   Low, Alfred D. *Jews in the Eyes of the Germans: From the Enlightenment to Imperial Germany.* Philadelphia: Institute for the Study of Human Issues, 1979.

See the annotation at entry 259.

670   Majer, Diemut. "Racial Inequality and the Nazification of the Law in Nazi Germany." *Israel Yearbook on Human Rights* 14 (1984): 111-119.

The author claims that racist ideas are not usually enacted as new laws but equated with similar sounding traditional concepts. Thus what appears as an expansion of the ethnic principle may not develop a status of rights for these groups but rather an annulment of human rights of the individual. The Nazi example illustrates this principle in which native populations were not only outside German legal order but beyond any legal order at all.

671   Mann, K. "Judicial Review and Fundamental Values: The Right to Counsel and Its Development in Israeli Law." *Tel Aviv University Law Review (Iyyunei Mishpat)* 13, 3 (1988): 557-612.

Mann distinguishes between the active protection of the right to counsel and a merely formal gesture. In the United States that right became prominent in the 1930s as the basis for individual freedom and liberty. Israeli law now faces a similar crisis.

672   Marx, Karl. "Die Heilige Famile." In *Historische - Kritische Gesamitausgabe*, Karl Marx and Frederick Engels, 173-388. Berlin: Marx-Engels Verlag, 1929.

See the annotation at entry 262.

673   Marx, Karl. "Zür Judenfrage." In *Historische-Kritische Gesamitausgabe*, Karl Marx and Frederick Engels, 576-606. Berlin: Marx-Engels Verlag, 1929.

See the annotation at entry 263.

674   Meislin, B. J. "Refusal to Testify as a Protected First Amendment Religious Right." *Jewish Law Annual* 1 (1978): 219-221.

See the annotation at entry 113.

675   Meron, Simha. "Freedom of Religion as Distinct from Freedom from Religion." *Israel Yearbook on Human Rights* 4 (1974): 219-240.

See the annotation at entry 264.

676   Meron, Theodor. *Human Rights Law-Making in the United Nations: A Critique of Instruments and Process.*   Oxford: Clarendon Press, 1986.

See the annotation at entry 371.

677   More, Daniel. "Film and Theatre Censorship in Israel." *Israel Yearbook on Human Rights* 9 (1979): 225-251.

According to More, since Britain established a Censorship Board in 1927 to ban subversive films and plays there has been no clear criteria for nomination of members.   He notes the practice of delegating authority to a subcommittee, but claims that this is not according to letter of the law.   He laments intimidation by public opinion and the lack of judicial review of the Board's decisions.   He, therefore, calls for its abolition.

678   Moskowitz, Moses. *International Concern with Human Rights.*   Dobbs Ferry, NY and Leiden, Netherlands: Oceana and Sijthoff, 1974.

The book describes and analyzes international concern with human rights violations, including data from cases involving Jews.

679   Moskowitz, Moses. "The Narrowing Horizons of United Nations Concern with Racial Discrimination." *Revue des Droits de l'Homme. Human Rights Journal* 4, 23 (1971): 278-292.

This article notes the exclusion of antisemitism from the catalogue of racial discrimination.

680   Moskowitz, Moses. *The Politics and Dynamics of Human Rights.*   Dobbs Ferry, NY: Oceana, 1968.

This study of the idea and practice of human rights includes references to the infringement of the rights of Jews.

681   Mosse, George L. "Jewish Emancipation: Between Bildung and Respectability." *The Jewish Response to German Culture From the Enlightenment to the Second World War*, eds. Jehuda Reinharz and Walter Schatzberg, 1-16. Hanover, NH: University Press of New England, 1985.

Mosse argues that the twin concepts of *Bildung* and *Sittlichkeit*, self-improvement and good manners, were impossible ideals for Jews.   While "liberated" by the philosphers of the Enlightenment into liberal politics, they could not accept the compromise offered by that liberation.   The humanistic ideal of individual, personal human rights inevitably conflicted with the Jewish desire to remain attached to an ancestral community and its traditions.   Mosse claims that antisemitism revealed the failure of a theory of rights to lead to Jewish integration into German society.

682   Moughrabi, Fouad and Zureik, Elia. *Different Scales of Justice: Arabs and Jews in Israel, Results of a National Survey*. Fouad Moughrabi and Elia Züreik, series eds., Occasional Paper 11. Kingston, Ontario: Near East Cultural and Educational Foundation of Canada, 1988.

This empirical study correlates ethnic and economic status with Israeli views on such human rights issues as equal access to justice, capital punishment, and equal treatment by the criminal system.

683   Muskat, Marion. "Judaisme et la 'Troisième Generation' des Droits." In *Judaisme et Droits de l'Homme*, ed. Emmanuel Hirsch, 207-214. Idéologies et Droits de l'Homme   B.01. Paris: Librairie des Libertés, 1984. French

See the annotation at entry 115.

684   Nahmani, Hayim Simha. *Human Rights in the Old Testament*. Tel Aviv: Joseph Chachik, 1964.

See the annotation at entry 116.

685   Pettiti, Louis E. "The Right to Leave and to Return in the USSR." *Israel Yearbook on Human Rights* 5 (1975): 264-275.

This article analyzes the refusal to allow Soviet Jews to emigrate as an infraction on the right to free movement.

686   Pierson, Christopher. "Marxism and Rights." In *Approaches to Marx*, eds. Mark Cowling and Lawrence Wilde, 172-184. Philadelphia: Open University Press, 1989.

See the annotation at entry 271.

687   Plaskow, Judith. *Standing Again At Sinai: Judaism From a Feminist Perspective*. San Francisco: Harper and Row, 1990.

See the annotation at entry 373.

688   Porter, Jack N., ed. *Genocide and Human Rights: A Global Anthology*. Washington, DC: University Press of America, 1982.

See the annotation at entry 016.

689   Pulzer, Peter. "Jewish Participation in Wilhelmine Politics." In *Jews and
       Germans From 1860-1933: The Problematic Symbiosis*, ed. David
       Bronsen, 78-99. Heidelberg: Carl Winter, 1979.

       See the annotation at entry 273.

690   Raab, Earl. "The Black Revolution and the Jewish Question." In *Black
       Anti-Semitism and Jewish Racism*, 15-41. New York: Richard W.
       Baron, 1969.

       Raab, like Marx before him, points to structural realities in
       American political and economic life that give rise to both a "Jewish
       Question" and a "Black Question." He shows how the problems
       both groups face grow out of the ethnic and racial tensions in
       America and how these must be addressed rather than the symptoms
       they cause.

691   Rabinovich, Itamar. "Anti-Semitism in the Muslim and Arab World." In
       Anti-Semitism and Human Rights, ed. Serge Liberman, 43-52, 81,
       83, 85-87. North Melbourne, Vic.: Australian Institute of Jewish
       Affairs, 1985.

       Surveying Arab attacks on Israel, Professor Rabinovich includes a
       consideration of the United Nation's condemnation of Zionism as
       racism, which, he suggests, was the result of a joint Soviet-Arab
       effort.   He contends that this denunciation of the Jewish people
       exonerates anti-Jewish behavior.   In response to questions he
       suggested that the Israelis, unlike the Arabs, have not racialized the
       conflict with the Palestinians and points to the Dayan Centre in Israel
       which has a special program to cultivate Arab-Jewish understanding.

692   Rabinowitz, Aaron K. "Human Rights Problems in the United States and
       in Israel." *Jewish Social Studies* 34 (1972): 207-242.

       The author compares several issues concerning civil liberties as they
       arise in America and in the State of Israel. The dynamics of such
       rights as those of voting, fair housing, due process, freedom of
       thought, religion, press and association differ when a society faces
       a real threat to its existence. Israel, whose Arab citizens often join
       with Israeli's political enemies and aid them when attacking the
       Israeli state, cannot afford to extend the same freedoms to those
       potential fifth-columnists that Americans can well afford to extend
       to its dissident citizens.

693   Radi, F. *Women's Rights*. Jerusalem: The Association for Civil Rights in
       Israel, 1989. Hebrew.

       See the annotation at entry 536.

694   Ragins, Sanford. *Jewish Responses to Anti-Semitism in Germany, 1870-1914: A Study in the History of Ideas.* Alumni Series. Cincinnati, OH: Union of American Hebrew Congregations, 1980.

The book describes how German opposition to Jews changed from opposing Jewish religion to opposing the assimilated, enlightened Jew. In the light of this change, Jewish liberals could no longer rely on the rights of citizens to protect them but needed a stronger case which some found in universal individual rights and others, Zionists, in the right to national independence.

695   Rakover, Nahum. "The Protection of Privacy in Jewish Law." *Israel Yearbook on Human Rights* 5 (1975): 169-80.

See the annotation at entry 505.

696   Ronen, Dov. *The Quest for Self-Determination.* New Haven, CT: Yale University Press, 1979.

The author analyzes the modern desire of ethnic and cultural groups to have self-determination. Both Jews and Israel provide examples of this.

697   Rosen-Zvi, Ariel. "The Place of the Woman in the Family in Jewish Law." In *Human Rights in Israel: Articles in Memory of Judge Haman Shelah,* ed. Ann Swersky, 109-151. Tel Aviv: Edanim and Yediot Aharonot, 1988. Hebrew.

See the annotation at entry 122.

698   Rotenstreich, Nathan. "For and Against Emancipation: The Bruno Bauer Controversy." *The Leo Baeck Institute Yearbook* 4 (1959): 3-36.

See the annotation at entry 279.

699   Rotenstreich, Nathan. *Jew and German Philosophy: The Polemics of Emancipation.* New York: Schocken, 1984.

See the annotation at entry 280.

700   Rotenstreich, Nathan. "Of Freedom." In his *Order and Might.* Albany, NY: State University of New York Press, 1988.

See the annotation at entry 405.

701   Rotenstreich, Nathan. "Of Justice." In his *Order and Might*, 107-134. Albany, NY: State University of New York Press, 1988.

See the annotation at entry 450.

702   Roth, John K., and Rubenstein, Richard L., eds. *Approaches to Auschwitz: The Holocaust and its Legacy*, Atlanta: John Knox, 1987.

The authors discuss the modern condition in which the exercise of fundamental rights is guaranteed only to a society's 'full members' and thus can be denied at the will of the political order.

703   Roth, Stephen J. "Anti-Semitism and International Law." *Israel Yearbook on Human Rights* 13 (1983): 208-225.

Roth comments that statements by many national and international bodies do not explicitly mention antisemitism as a form of racism unlike their treatment of apartheid.   Since no international protections exist against group libel Jews face discrimination if they are not given a specific group identity. An illustration of the problem occurs in the denial of the Holocaust as a crime that requires specific redress but one for which none has yet been created.

704   Roth, Stephen J. "The Legal Fight Against Anti-Semitism -- The National Aspect." In *Anti-Semitism and Human Rights*, ed. Serge Liberman, 157-164. North Melbourne, Vic.: Australian Institute of Jewish Affairs, 1985.

Roth notes the absence of antisemitism as a form of racism in the international instruments which deal with human rights and suggests the reasons leading to that absence.   He sees challenges to the use of traditional legal means to respond to such antisemitic forms as distortion of historical truth about the holocaust and the disguising of antisemitism as anti-Zionism.   He calls for a reappraisal of the laws on human rights to make explicit mention of antisemitism which destroys the rights and dignity of one entire group of human beings, the Jews.

705   Roth, Stephen J. "The Roots of Modern Anti-Semitism and the New Anti-Semitism." In *Anti-Semitism and Human Rights*, ed. Serge Liberman, 9-14. North Melbourne, Vic.: Australian Institute of Jewish Affairs, 1985.

The author considers the third period in the history of antisemitism: that ushered in by the philosophers of human rights.   This new philosophical emphasis on emancipation and human equality led to a new Judeophobia--racial antisemitism.   After the Nazi period, however, a new rationale for denying Jews equal rights was required since neither religion nor race would suffice. By 1973, the author suggests, a new anti-semitism arose--that of terrorism directed against the existence of the Jewish national body.

706   Rozenblum, Serge-Allain. "La Violation des Droits des Juifs en USSR." In *Judaisme et Droits de l'Homme*, ed. Emmanuel Hirsch, 169-173. Idéologies et Droits de l'Homme   B.01. Paris: Librairie des Libertés, 1984. French.

According to the author, the status of the Jews in the Soviet Union demonstrates the problems of a modern minority. They can neither affirm their identity fully nor deny their status as a minority. Such a condition violates their human rights.

707   Rubin, Benjamin. "PLO Violence and Legitimate Combatancy: A Response to Professor Green." *Israel Yearbook on Human Rights* 19 (1989): 167-185.

The author offers a rebuttal of the claim that PLO activities can be construed as legitimate actions by combatants rather than as terrorism. He contends that the PLO and its activities have never been construed as legitimate combatants in the Israeli law.

708   Rubinstein, Amnon. "The Right to Marriage." *Israel Yearbook on Human Rights* 3 (1973): 233-255.

The author discusses the secularizing of the right to marriage, but suggests that every limitation on the capacity to marry conflicts with freedom of conscience, the rule of law, and democratic values. Nevertheless, he claims that Israel obstructs the right by depriving specific religious groups of the right and limiting it on religious grounds. The evasions of these restrictions, he thinks, weaken the very institutions they were meant to serve.

709   Rubinstein, Amnon. "The Struggle Over a Bill of Rights for Israel." In *Constitutionalism: The Israeli and American Experiences*, ed. Daniel J. Elazar, 139-142. Lanham, MD: University Press of America, 1990.

See the annotation at entry 286.

710   Rudolph, Harold. "The Judicial Review of Administrative Detention Orders in Israel." *Israel Yearbook on Human Rights* 14 (1984): 148-181.

The author studies the detention of Meir Kahane in 1980. He notes the argument that Kahane's threat to security was so dangerous that there was no other way of preventing the danger other than his detention.   Nevertheless, he offers a critique of this process of judgment and illustrates his concern by looking at other such cases.

711   Runes, Dagobert G., ed. *Karl Marx: A World Without Jews*. New York: The Philosophical Library, 1960.

See the annotation at entry 287.

712   Samuels, Shimon.   "Anti-Semitism: The Abiding Prejudice."   In *Anti-Semitism and Human Rights*, ed. Serge Liberman, 15-18, 35-36. North Melbourne, Vic.: Australian Institute of Jewish Affairs, 1985.

See the annotation at entry 382.

713   Schneider, Hagi. *Freedom of Religion in Israel*.   Jerusalem: The Association for Civil Rights in Israel, 1990. Hebrew.

See the annotation at entry 334.

714   Schoenberg, Harris O. "Limits of Self-determination." *Israel Yearbook on Human Rights* 6 (1976): 91-103.

The essay studies the problems in granting an absolute right to self-determination.

715   Shamir, Michal. "Political Toleration and Administration in the Israeli Community." In *Human Rights in Israel: Articles in Memory of Judge Haman Shelah*, ed. Ann Swersky, 81-93. Tel Aviv: Edanim and Yediot Aharonot, 1988. Hebrew.

The author notes the interplay of tolerance understood as a positive value and the problems raised by demonstrations for unpopular ideas, such as the pro-Nazi demonstrations in Skokie, IL. She recognizes the limits of tolerance, even in a democracy such as Israel, when faced with clear and present danger. In particular she notes that Israel is caught between the on-going conflict with its Arab neighbors and its tradition of liberal politics. While the natural condition is not that of tolerance, the intellectual and judicial elite have the responsibility of ensuring the possibility for tolerance.

716   Shapira, Amos. "Human Right to Die: Israeli and Jewish Legal Perspectives." *Israel Yearbook on Human Rights* 7 (1977): 127-138.

See the annotation at entry 127.

717   Shapira, Amos. "Legislative and Judicial Law-Making Concerning Educational Liberty and Equality: Some Israeli Constitutional Law Perspectives." *Israel Yearbook on Human Rights* 9 (1979): 181-189.

The author notes Israel's impressive record of defending individual freedoms. He examines in detail a 1971 case that entailed the necessity of positing a normative freedom for parental choice of school.

718   Shapiro-Libai, Nitza. "The Concept of Sex Equality: The UN Decade for Women." *Israel Yearbook on Human Rights* 11 (1981): 106-132.

This essay reviews the modern challenge raised by the idea of sexual equality and gives examples from Israeli experience.

719   Shapiro-Libai, Nitza. "The Right to Abortion." *Israel Yearbook on Human Rights* 5 (1975): 120-140.

The author argues that the right to abortion derives from freedom of choice whether to bear or beget a child. Individuals have a fundamental right to shape their lives and that of their families. Israel's restrictions of the right to abortion derive from a restrictive and unwarranted concern and do not preserve human rights.

720   Shelach, Chaman P. "Freedom of Conscience and Freedom of Heart." In *Civil Rights in Israel*, ed. Ruth Gavison, 85-115. Jerusalem: The Association for Civil Rights in Israel, 1982. Hebrew.

See the annotation at entry 400.

721   Sheleff, Leon. "Conscientious Dissent from the Law." In *Civil Rights in Israel*, ed. Ruth Gavison, 117-151. Jerusalem: The Association for Civil Rights in Israel, 1982. Hebrew.

See the annotation at entry 347.

722   Sheleff, Leon. "Rabbi Captain Goldman's Yarmulke, Freedom of Religion and Conscience, and Civil (Military) Disobedience." *Israel Yearbook on Human Rights* 17 (1987): 197-221.

The author claims that the prohibition upheld constitutes a serious erosion of the constitutional right to freedom of religion for minorities. He claims that it was not professional judgment as to the immediate needs of military discipline, but mere adherence to the dry lifeless letter of the law, activated only because of an angry reaction by the prosecutor.

723   Sherwin, Byron L. "The Sanctity of Life in an Age of Violence." In his *In Partnership with God: Contemporary Jewish Law and Ethics*, 169-180. Syracuse: Syracuse University Press, 1990.

See the annotation at entry 130.

724   Shestreet, Shimon. "The Scope of Judicial Review of National Security Considerations in Free Speech and other Areas: The Israeli Perspective." *Israel Yearbook on Human Rights* 18 (1988): 35-47.

The author discusses the problem of protecting civil rights in a time of continuing national emergency. He claims that the government has failed to show due restraint in exercising its regulatory power.

725   Shestreet, Shimon. "Some Reflections on Freedom of Conscience in Israel." *Israel Yearbook on Human Rights* 4 (1974): 194-218.

The author considers the problem of separating religion and state in Israel. He nevertheless concludes that the imposition of religious norms may have a pragmatic rationale. See his response to the critique of Simha Meron, entry 264, pp. 241-44. This essay is also found, in slightly different form as "Freedom of Conscience and Religion in Israel" in entry 020, 179-192.

726   Shnit, Dan. "The Foetus as a Legal Person Under Israeli Law." *Israel Yearbook on Human Rights* 16 (1986): 308-320.

See the annotation at entry 486.

727   Shnit, Dan. "Limitations on the Rights of the Mentally Ill to be Heard: Exception or Error?" *Israel Yearbook on Human Rights* 12 (1982): 195-213.

This essay looks at the need to extend a theory of human rights to even those traditionally excluded from exercising those rights. While not referring to Jewish precedent which does indeed place liabilities to those with impaired faculties, this essay shows how a modern consciousness forces Jews to rethink their theory of human rights.

728   Sigler, Jay A. *Minority Rights: A Comparative Analysis*. Bernard K. Johnpoll, Series ed., Contributions in Political Science   104. Westport, CT: Greenwood, 1983.

Sigler uses the Jews as primary examples of a minority whose rights must be respected. Soviet Jews are discussed in relationship to the right of movement. He discusses Nazism and its abuse of Jewish rights and genocidal attempt in several passages. His analysis of religious discrimination in the United States uses the Jews and Seventh Day Adventists as examples of those who have not done well under Supreme Court interpretations of the Constitution. He suggests that much "relatively unregulated" religious discrimination occurs throughout the top management levels and in the private life of Americans. He also uses the example of religious segregation and a quota system for admission to private schools as evidence of abuse of human rights in England.

729   Slonim, Shlomo, ed. *The Constitutional Bases of Political and Social Change in the United States*. Westport, CT: Praeger, 1990.

Despite its title this book includes selections devoted to Israeli constitutionalism as well as to American Jews and their benefit from the American constitution. See entries 385, 454, 590, 640, 661, 668.

730   Sorkin, David Jan. "The Invisible Community: Emancipation, Secular Culture, and Jewish Identity in the Writings of Berthold Auerbach." In *The Jewish Response to German Culture From the Enlightenment to the Second World War*, eds. Jehuda Reinharz and Walter Schatzberg, 100-119. Hanover, NH: University Press of New England, 1985.

See the annotation at entry 294.

731   Sorkin, David Jan. *The Transformation of German Jewry, 1780-1840*. New York: Oxford University Press, 1987.

See the annotation at entry 295.

732   Stanek, Edward. *Human Rights: A Selected Bibliography of Monographs, Essays, Serials and Basic Compilations of Documents and Bibliographies Pertinent to International Protection of Human Rights.* Public Administration Series: Bibliography   P21104. Monticello, IL: Vance Bibliographies, 1987.

See the annotation at entry 030.

733   Stein, Gustav, ed. *Menschenrechte in Israel und Deutschland: Ein Syumposium der Gesellschaft zür Forderung der Wissenschaftlichen Zusammenarbeit mit der Universitat Tel Aviv (Human Rights in Israel and Germany: A Symposium of the Society for the Advancement of Scientific Cooperation with Tel Aviv University).* Cologne: Nottbeck, 1978. German.

This anthology includes a discussion of human rights in both Israel and Germany in the contemporary period. It shows how the theory of human rights in the modern world focuses on Jews and Jewish issues and how cooperation among nations can address this issue.

734   Stendel, Ori. "The Rights of the Arab Minority in Israel." *Israel Yearbook on Human Rights* 1 (1971): 134-155.

This article focuses on the political rights of the Arabs. The author claims that principle of equal rights is set in the Zionist vision and that the Arabs are granted many specific freedoms. Nevertheless he admits that the ideal of equality has not yet been achieved.

735   Susser, Baruch. "A Proposed Constitution for Israel." In *Constitutionalism: The Israeli and American Experiences*, ed. Daniel J. Elazar, 179-189. Lanham, MD: University Press of America, 1990.

Susser's proposal takes account of the several religious issues that intersect questions of general human and civil rights. He admits that calling Israel a Jewish state violates the American sense of First Amendment rights. Nevertheless he calls for a judicious balance rather than a wall of separation between religious and civil concerns. He defends legislating Sabbath observance for the nation as a whole. While the origin of such observance may be religious, the Sabbath as such, he contends, expresses the national cultural heritage of the Jewish people and may, therefore, be imposed on the nation as a whole.

736   Tabory, Ephraim. "Religious Rights as a Social Problem in Israel." *Israel Yearbook on Human Rights* 11 (1981): 256-271.

See the annotation at entry 300.

737   Tarcov, Nathan and Thomas L. Pangle. "Epilogue: Leo Strauss and the History of Political Philosophy." In *History of Political Philosophy*, eds. Leo Strauss and Joseph Cropsey, 907-938. Chicago: University of Chicago Press, 1987.

See the annotation at entry 301.

738   Traer, Robert. "Jews." In his *Faith in Human Rights: Support in Religious Traditions for a Global Struggle*, 99-110. Washington, DC: Georgetown University Press, 1991.

See the annotation at entry 302.

739   Van Dyke, Kermon. *Human Rights, Ethnicity, and Discrimination*. Contributions in Ethnic Studies   10. Westport, CT: Greenwood, 1985.

This study discusses prohibitions on proselytism in Israel as a restriction on freedom of religion and interprets the use of the millet system as meaning that individuals are treated differently depending on their religion.

740   Vazquez, Modsesto Seara. "The Soviet Jewish Minority and the Right to Leave." *Israel Yearbook on Human Rights* 4 (1974): 302-307.

The author provides a definition and typology of minorities distinguishing between dominating, dominated, and nationalistic minorities and those seeking independence, autonomy, integration, emigration. He realizes the limitations on the effectiveness of the appeal to law, but that appeal can create the public opinion needed to effect change. Soviet Jewry provides an example of one type of minority.

741   Vincent, R. J. *Human Rights and International Relations*. Cambridge: Cambridge University Press and The Royal Institute of International Affairs, 1986.

The author uses the case of Soviet Jewish dissidents to illustrate the differences between how Western nations view human rights and how those rights appear to members of the Eastern Block. He also uses the case of United Nation's condemnation of Israel and Zionism to show that it is politics rather than a concern for human rights which animates the agenda of human rights issues in that body.

742   Vital, David. *The Future of the Jews*.   Cambridge, MA: Harvard University Press, 1990.

Sketching what he sees as the waning of the Jewish nation, Vital contrasts the Western European Jewish legacy of humanism, an optimistic assumption of certain universal rights, and a hopeful view for future progress, with the world view of Jews outside of the West. In Israel the political division leads to disastrous internal struggle, and, in the diaspora, leads to alienation from Judaism and the modern State of Israel. The view of human rights Jews hold seems to Vital tied to their acceptance or rejection of the heritage of the Enlightenment, a heritage which he thinks will lead to the failure of the Jewish people.

743   Vorspan, Albert. "Blacks and Jews." In *Black Anti-Semitism and Jewish Racism*, 143-188. New York: Richard W. Baron, 1969.

Vorspan decries the use of slogans such as "black antisemitism" or "Jewish racism." Instead he argues that Jews and blacks must move away from both liberalism and colonialism to address the root problems of American life. Using antisemitism as an excuse to disengage from social activism, he thinks, misses the point. Symptoms are less important than the causes of hatred, violence, and frustration.

744   Vorspan, Albert. "Civil Liberties." In his *Great Jewish Debates and Dilemmas: Jewish Perspectives in Conflict in the Eighties*, 35-52. New York: Union of American Hebrew Congregations, 1980.

Vorspan surveys problems arising from conflicting values in civil liberties. He looks at occasions on which Jews and Nazis have clashed and investigates the issues of the right to privacy and the right to freedom from censorship.

745   Warhaftig, Itamar. "The Ethics of Using Prisoners for Experimentation." *Techumin: Torah, Society, and State: Compendium of Halakha* 1 (1980): 530-536.

See the annotation at entry 406.

746   Weiler, Gershon. "On Freedom of Religion and Worship." In *Human Rights in Israel: Articles in Memory of Judge Haman Shelah*, ed. Ann Swersky, 22-35. Tel Aviv: Edanim and Yediot Aharonot, 1988. Hebrew.

See the annotation at entry 140.

747   Weiler, Gershon. "Religion and Human Rights in Israel." *Index on Censorship* 5 (October 1983): 7-9.

See the annotation at entry 394.

748   Weisbard, Alan J. "On the Bioethics of Jewish Law: The Case of Karen Quinlan." *Israel Law Review* 14 (1979): 337-368.

See the annotation at entry 490.

749   Weltsch, Robert. "Introduction." *Leo Baeck Institute Yearbook* 4 (1959): ix-xxvi.

See the annotation at entry 384.

750   Wyschogrod, Michael. "Religion and International Human Rights: A Jewish Perspective." In *Formation of Social Policy in the Catholic and Jewish Traditions*, eds. Eugene J. Fisher and Daniel F. Polish, 123-141. South Bend, IN: University of Notre Dame Press, 1980.

See the annotation at entry 144.

751   Yannai, Nathan. "Politics and Constitution-Making in Israel: Ben-Gurion's Position in the Constitutional Debate Following the Foundation of the State." In *Constitutionalism: The Israeli and American Experiences*, ed. Daniel J. Elazar, 101-114. Lanham, MD: University Press of America, 1990.

The author traces how Ben Gurion's desire to balance a state that preserved individual rights with a state representing Jewish religion shaped his political position on the creation of an Israeli constitution.

752   Zeltner, Zeev. "The Struggle for Human Rights and Its Implications." In *Of Law and Man: Essays in Honor of Haim Cohn*, ed. Shlomo Shoham, 47-57. New York: Sabra, 1971.

See the annotation at entry 146.

Author Index

The index that follows contains only the primary authors or editors appearing in citations or in the Introductory Survey. References to the Introductory Survey are indicated by page number; references to the Bibliographical Survey are indicated by citation number.

Title Index

The references in this index are to the citation numbers of entries in which the title occurs as the primary citation; anthologies are noted only if they are the primary citation.

Subject Index

This index includes subjects discussed in the Introductory Survey and in the citations but not included as specific rubrics in the Biographical Survey. References to the former are indicated by page number, to the later by citation number.

About the Author

S. DANIEL BRESLAUER is Professor in the Department of Religious Studies at The University of Kansas. His other books include *Covenant and Community in Modern Judaism* (Greenwood Press, 1989), *Modern Jewish Morality: A Bibliographical Survey* (Greenwood Press, 1986), and *Contemporary Jewish Ethics: A Bibliographical Survey* (Greenwood Press, 1985).